**Citizens
of Soil**

Drizzle

OLIVE OIL-INFUSED RECIPES
FROM ACROSS THE MEDITERRANEAN

SARAH FULTON VACHON

MITCHELL BEAZLEY

For Maria,
a dear friend who became family,
and opened up our world to *olive* this.

First published in Great Britain in 2026 by Mitchell Beazley,
an imprint of
Octopus Publishing Group Ltd
Carmelite House, 50 Victoria Embankment, London EC4Y 0DZ
www.octopusbooks.co.uk

An Hachette UK Company
www.hachette.co.uk

The authorized representative in the EEA is Hachette Ireland,
8 Castlecourt Centre, Dublin 15, D15 XTP3, Ireland
(email: info@hbgi.ie)

Text Copyright © Sarah Fulton Vachon 2026
Photography © Octopus Publishing Group Ltd 2026
Design and layout Copyright © Octopus Publishing Group Ltd 2026

Additional Picture Credits:
Courtesy Citizens of Soil 4bl, 4br, 11, 13tr, 28, 40
Courtesy Harriet Clare 13br, 13Bl
Courtesy Marly Zemsta 4tl, 28,164
© Ola Smit 4tr, 7, 8, 10, 28, 40, 63, 98, 130, 164

Distributed in the US by Hachette Book Group
1290 Avenue of the Americas, 4th and 5th Floors,
New York, NY 10104

Distributed in Canada by Canadian Manda Group,
664 Annette St., Toronto, Ontario, Canada M6S 2C8

ISBN: 978-1-8460-1619-6
eISBN: 978-18460-1620-2

A CIP catalogue record for this book is available from the British Library.

Printed and bound in China.

10 9 8 7 6 5 4 3 2 1

Commissioning Editor Jeannie Stanley
Creative Director Jonathan Christie
Design Intern Mominah Aslam
Senior Editor Alex Stetter
Photographer Ola Smit
Home Economist Annie Rigg
Props Stylist Louie Waller
Senior Production Manager Katherine Hockley

FSC
www.fsc.org
MIX
Paper | Supporting
responsible forestry
FSC® C008047

Key

 Spring

 Summer

 Autumn

 Winter

Contents

Introduction

Most people tend to think of olive oil as something for drizzling over salad or serving as a dip with bread. But I like to think of it like this: poured over vanilla ice cream, dropped in a dirty martini, coating a good piece of fish and forming part of my skincare regime. I dream in liquid gold. That's because I'm an olive oil sommelier – a professional trained to distinguish great products from the merely good or, it must be said, the fake.

I have the privilege of travelling the world and working directly with some of the best artisan producers to source the sort of extra virgin olive oils that really get people excited. And I'm here to make new converts. But I'm not alone in this – like wine, extra virgin olive oil (EVOO) attracts not only those who are into gastronomy, it also draws in those who like to understand the nuances of terroir, or the sense of place. It's that whole connection with nature: how it has an impact on flavour and the ways in which those flavours change from harvest to harvest.

Beyond my sommelier studies, I've learned more about olive oil from taking part in its production and hearing first-hand from the award-winning makers who perfect this craft. My husband and I started Citizens of Soil in 2020 to bring the EVOO produced by our close family friends in Crete to the UK, but it quickly became much bigger than that. Our focus on small-batch producers who farm in harmony with nature, prioritizing the health of both people and planet, created a shift in us and the category.

The recipes we've collected for you here come from some of these very producers, educators and mentors who have helped me along the way. I hope you see this book as your jumping off point into all things *extra*. May it surprise you, delight you, change you and heal you.

Welcome to the wonderful world of olive oil.

Olive my best,

Sarah

The Olive Tree

What better way to come to an understanding of olive oil than to get, quite literally, to its roots? Olive trees have been cultivated for millennia by many civilizations. They are celebrated for their resilience, and their longevity has led to them being referred to as the 'eternal tree'. I've put my arms around some of these 'monument' trees that are thousands of years old and still bearing fruit – and for all we know, they will live forever.

One ancient example, in the Palestinian village of Al-Walaja, near Bethlehem, is at least 4,000 years old, and said to be the oldest olive tree in the world. These trees are tough and able to survive harsh conditions, so it's little wonder that their gnarled shapes are such a distinctive presence in Mediterranean landscapes.

Olive leaves and stones dating back to around 12,000 BC have been uncovered all around the Mediterranean basin. Cultivation of olive trees likely started with the Phoenicians in Asia Minor, but then flowed over to the Greek islands and beyond. The ancient Greeks played their part in continuing the spread, followed by the Romans. Then came the Spanish, who took their beloved trees to the New World, planting them across the Americas. Their 'Mission' cultivar, so called because it was originally planted by missionaries, is grown in California and Mexico to this day.

The olive tree we're now familiar with, *Olea Europaea*, actually started out as a bush, but human intervention transformed it into a tree over time. Even today, when left to their own devices, olive trees will begin to turn themselves back into a bush, with shoots coming up from the base.

There's a rich history intertwined with olive trees' presence as pillars of the landscape, with a significance that goes far beyond the culinary. The olive tree has been a symbol of peace since antiquity, and its roots in some of the world's most contested and war-torn regions is not lost on the communities that hold it dear.

In ancient times, the olive wreath was a part of the Olympic Games, serving as the winner's crown. Today this symbol adorns currency, flags, government badges, buildings, statues and medals – a continuing sign of peace and reconciliation.

ATHENA'S TREE

The Greeks love to tell the story of how Athens got its name. According to Greek mythology, both Athena, the goddess of wisdom, and Poseidon, the god of the sea, wanted to be the patron deity of this flourishing new city. To settle the dispute, they were asked to offer a gift to the city, and its citizens would decide which was best.

For his gift, Poseidon struck the ground with his trident and a salt-water spring appeared – a symbol of his naval and military power. For her gift, Athena knelt on the ground and planted a seed, from which an olive tree emerged full of fruit.

The olive tree – which could provide everything from timber for construction and olives for food to oil for lighting lamps and healing – won out. Athena became the guardian of the city, which took her name, and the olive tree became its revered symbol.

You can find this legacy alive in the sacred olive tree planted on the Acropolis, the city's ancient citadel. Said to be a descendant of Athena's tree, it was burned when the Persians sacked the city in 480 BC, only to grow back from its charred roots. It was badly damaged during World War II, but fortunately, the American School of Archaeology rescued a branch. The tree at the Acropolis today comes from that cutting.

Olive Oil
A Brief History

Some 8,000 years ago, oil pressed from olives first began to appear in the eastern Mediterranean and Levant region. Freshly picked olives are intensely bitter and it takes a lot of treatment – either curing, brining or crushing – to make them palatable. But some brave soul thought eating them was a good idea, and olive oil evenually became part of daily life.

In ancient times, it was applied to the body, then scraped off with a special tool to ensure all dirt and impurities were removed. Olive oil went on to be used in soaps and beauty treatments, and is still used in skincare today. It also was burned as fuel in lamps – quite literally being a light in the darkness. Olive oil has also long been celebrated for its medicinal benefits – Hippocrates called it 'the great healer'. This liquid gold soon became a valuable commodity that was traded to far-flung places. Olive oil helped feed and fuel the Greek and Roman empires as they expanded over time.

FAKES AND FRAUDS

Olive oil is prized for its many applications, but it's likely that our obsession with it has made the industry around it ripe for exploitation and corruption. What's sometimes sold as 'olive oil' can be low quality at best, or at worst a mixture of downright dubious origins. Some products sold as olive oil can consist largely of other, cheaper, types of oil, with a little extra virgin thrown in for aroma, colour and flavour.

This is not a recent phenomenon. Evidence of fraud dates back to the ancient Romans, who across their empire implemented anti-fraud and traceability measures to root out deception. In Rome today, you can visit Monte Testaccio, an enormous ancient man-made hill of broken olive oil pots. Stamped with their origin, they were broken to stop them being re-used for selling lower-quality oils at the original high price. This hill stands as a monument to the importance we have always placed on provenance.

The social impact of the industry on farmers and honest producers can't be avoided either. They are squeezed out by middlemen, who fragment supply chains, flood the market with fake products or mixed bulk oils, and effectively steal any tangible profits. From a lack of clarity all the way to outright fraud, ambiguity lies at the heart of the issue. Transparency is the only solution. If a brand is not forthcoming with information, that's a red flag. So before buying extra virgin olive oil, see my guide on pages 16–17.

PAST AND PRESENT

While small-scale artisans continue to do much of the farming and harvesting of olives by hand, the days of the donkey pulling the stone to crush the olives are (mostly) gone, as are the traditional presses. Being nearly impossible to keep clean, they were abandoned in favour of stainless-steel machines to ensure fresher, cleaner and defect-free oils. As a producer explained to me once: 'It's safe to say the ancient Greeks were not consuming extra virgin.' The modern practices in place today have raised the bar substantially in most cases. And quality standards – however broad those of us in the speciality space might feel they are – mean we're enjoying better olive oil than ever. Even if there's still a way to go…

Our First Harvest Day

We drive down the rocky dirt road to a hillside with sweeping views over Crete. The Amargiotakis family calls this grove Stavros, which means 'cross' in Greek. There we have a handful of people to help us, a mixture of friends plus some workers hired from the village. Increasingly, finding labour is one of the biggest challenges for traditional groves. Harvesting olives is hard, physical work that not many people want to do – and as many of the harvest workers are locked into larger farm projects, finding labour is even harder for small producers.

As we unpack, everyone moves as if on autopilot. They've all done this before. On a traditional grove – particularly hillside or mountain groves – the work is mostly done by hand, as the larger machines can't get in. It starts with setting out nets on the ground under the trees to catch the fruit. There is a particular strategy and order to setting them out, and one person takes the lead.

Once the nets are out, it's time to harvest the fruit. How this is done depends on where you are and what quality the producer ultimately wants the oil to be. You want to be firm enough to get the olives, but gentle enough so as not to bruise them or step all over them. Sometimes picking is done exclusively by 'milking' the branches, which means pulling the olives off by hand or with small tools. This typically involves teams with ladders, but occasionally individuals crawl into the trees, something I love to do, though it's slow going. At other times picking is done with long electric rakes (sometimes called 'tree ticklers'), which brush or spin around to release the olives.

Of course, more mechanical processes can replace people power. Provided a grove is not on the side of a mountain and a grower has the means, it's possible to bring in tractors with an upside-down umbrella attachment, which circle around the trees, shaking them and catching the olives, saving you all the fuss with the nets.

Once all the fruit is out of the trees, it is rolled across the nets and funnelled into piles, which are then sorted by hand to remove twigs and leaves. The olives are then transferred to baskets or small plastic crates and loaded onto the truck for the mill.

NOW TO THE MILL

Harvesting, of course, is only part one of the day. Now, as a producer, you say goodbye to your workers (or most of them), and drive your olives to the mill. If you have your own mill, you're in luck. You can take the olives there for pressing in small batches right away, so you're turning the fruit into fat as quickly as possible to maximize freshness.

If, like Maria and Dimitris, you don't have your own mill, you might have to wait your turn outside a commercial or cooperative mill. This can mean spending hours waiting well into the night, or even until the next day, for your slot. This is far from ideal. Milling on the same day as harvesting is essential for producing the best quality oil, as the olives start to ferment the moment they're picked. Fortunately for us, Maria and Dimitris harvest earlier in the season than most in their area, so we can get a slot at the mill right away.

We pour our olives into a big sorting container, and they go up a conveyor belt, which has a fan to blow away the leaves. (These, by the way, make an excellent mulch.) The olives then go into what I call their spa: first, they are sprayed with water, then they are drained and finally they are air-dried.

Next, the olives are put into a machine – often a hammer mill – or passed through a series of rotating blades and crushed. Then they move on to the malaxer, which kneads and mixes the crushed olive paste. Once it looks like a tapenade and the first gloss of oil starts to show (usually after less than 30 minutes), it's time

to separate out the oil from the leftover mash. Depending on your kit here, the mixture now goes through one or sometimes two centrifuges to separate solids from liquids, but essentially we're all trying to get it down to just the oil as quickly as possible. No water, no olive parts.

Modern machines will let you control the temperature, to ensure the oil doesn't get over 27°C (80°F). The whole process usually creates heat naturally, and some heat is necessary to enable the extraction to occur, but a good miller will watch the time, temperature and movements throughout this production, optimizing steps to ensure the highest quality while getting the optimal amount of oil.

What comes out of the spout here is olive oil obtained directly from olives and solely by mechanical means. No heat, no chemicals. Unless the olives were in terrible shape – or the mill was not clean – what you've likely just made is an unfiltered virgin oil. Now, to get the oil its 'extra' grade requires a lab and sensory analysis – which we'll get into more later.

Checklist for a Stand-Out EVOO

Over the years, I've gone to many olive harvests across the Mediterranean and learned a huge amount from working alongside some of the world's most talented producers. Here's what the best oils have in common, according to the people who make them:

BEAUTIFUL FRUIT

Picture-perfect olives, without bruises, mould, fungus or spots from bugs. Most of the best producers pick out the best fruit, often by hand. Every olive can contribute to a better – or worse – final oil. Be selective here.

GOOD FARMING PRACTICES

The olives have not been over-watered for volume, but aren't wrinkled up from drought. It's tricky balance to strike, and increasingly hard for non-irrigated groves due to the climate. Also, biodiversity and healthy soils make for happy, more resilient, trees.

THE RIGHT TIMING

It's both an art and a science to pick the best moment for harvest, depending on what flavour profile you're after. For intensity, this typically means harvesting earlier in the season, around late September and October, and for more delicate oils, around December.

HARVESTING STYLE

Whatever way the producer chooses, it needs to cause as little damage to the fruit as possible. And the fruit need to be picked from the tree – olives that have already fallen on the ground days before are not harvested.

TIME TO MILL

One of the most crucial parts of this whole process. You want the shortest time between picking the fruit and putting it through the mill. Half an hour is the stuff of legends, but not always feasible. Within 2–5 hours is top tier, but same-day is also great if the olives are kept cool, out of the sun and stored in a way they can breathe.

IMMACULATE MILLING

'Hygiene in the mill is fundamental, if not key,' says Ana Cardoso, co-owner of Tratturo de Fronteira in Portugal. I don't care how romantic the old-school presses are, you want a milling outfit that prioritizes sanitation and attention to detail. Decisions are made here to make sure that what comes out of the spout represents the whole year's worth of effort.

FILTERING

All that vibrancy and sensation straight out of the spout is great, but it won't last. You need to remove the sediment for the oil to have any meaningful shelf-life, because every tiny bit you leave in there causes the oil to degrade faster – even if it looks and tastes better in those first few weeks when it's unfiltered.

PACKAGING

This must block out light and air. Certain plastics, such as PET (polyethylene terephthalate) and HDPE (high-density polyethylene), are permeable to air, so need an impermeable layer such as you find in a baby-food pouch or bag-in-box wine. At Citizens of Soil, we've done testing on packaging and quality over time. You need a robust material to hold up to EVOO.

STORING

The best producers don't just stop when the oil is in bottle. They ensure it's kept away from air, heat and light – even during transportation. Yes, it costs us more to ship oil in temperature-controlled containers, but letting it bake on a hot summer day in the back of a truck isn't worth it if you're ruthless on quality.

Grades of Olive Oil

The ancient Romans began the world's biggest man-made forest project, spreading olive trees across the Mediterranean basin. Their principal plantations – in Andalucía, Tunisia and Puglia – are still among the biggest producing regions in the world today. And the system the Romans used to formalize the different quality grades of olive oil is not far off from the framework we use now (minus the lab tests).

When it comes to olive oil categories, it's important to know how we get to 'extra'. So it's worth understanding this simple breakdown: all olives start off green. As they mature, their colour darkens. Unlike red and white grapes for wine, there are not two different types of olives. A rule of thumb is that the greener the olives, the more intense their flavour, so the higher the quality they are deemed to have.

That said, some varieties benefit from not being overly 'green'. Some will end up entirely too bitter and downright unpalatable – so early harvest doesn't guarantee a delicious EVOO.

Today, the International Olive Council has made classifications around olive oil which relate to both its chemical and organaleptic properties. Let's break down that framework, starting with the best.

EXTRA VIRGIN

Flawless 100% olive juice. This is the oil extracted without added heat over 27°C (80°F) or chemical means, and produced through a mechanical process of crushing, grinding or pressing. It must also have low acidity (measured as free fatty acid) of less than 0.8g per 100g, usually expressed as 0.8%. By definition, it must also be without detectable defects.

VIRGIN OLIVE OIL

Good, but not great. Although produced in the same way as extra virgin, so without heat or chemicals, it has a higher acidity (up to 2%) and some flaws. It's a good option for cooking, and it retains some of its nutrients.

OLIVE OIL

A refined oil that is not what it claims to be. It's a blend of refined oils that have undergone additional processing that includes bleaching, deodorizing and the use of solvents to make it fit for human consumption. The end result is odourless, colourless and tasteless. To fix that, it's typically mixed with a little extra virgin olive oil to enhance the aroma, flavour and appearance.

LAMPANTE

Meaning literally 'lamp oil', as that's all it's good for, this term is the greatest insult you can give to an olive oil. It needs to be further refined to be even considered fit for human consumption, or is used for non-edible purposes.

Comparing extra virgin olive oil and regular olive oil is like comparing freshly-squeezed orange juice with a carbonated soft drink. One comes from fresh fruit and provides nutrition on multiple levels, the other is a highly-processed, lifeless product made at a much lower cost.

What to avoid or ignore

There are some unscrupulous (or sometimes ignorant) people out there who hype up inferior products. It deceives customers, breaks down trust and cuts into the livelihood of quality producers who do things right. Watch out for the following...

Avoid

DECEPTIVE NAMING
Bulk commodity brands use misleading words, such as 'pure', 'light' and the super-shameful 'extra light' to describe their products, which infuriates me no end. These words are just another way of saying that the oil is refined, meaning that it has much less flavour and far fewer nutrients than extra virgin olive oil. 'Light' simply refers to the colour, a sure sign that an oil contains less good stuff; it does not mean it contains fewer calories than extra virgin olive oil. Again, the key word to look for is 'virgin'.

CLEAR CONTAINERS
Light degrades olive oil – it's as simple as that. Even exposure over a short time causes a breakdown in quality. So why would you ever package it in clear glass? I've seen producers at some stunning groves do this and asked them about it. The answer is sometimes ignorance, but mostly they want the shoppers to see the colour of the oil. They will give me a line about how they sell the bottle in a box or say to keep it in a dark pantry, but that's just not good enough.

BIG, BOLD CLAIMS WITHOUT PROOF
Extra virgin olive oil has countless benefits, some of which are only now being uncovered. But be wary of businesses making claims that their particular EVOO has more health benefits than others without showing you proof, such as certifications, the EU health claim stamp and lab analysis results. Beware of brands that make vague statements about 'youthful skin', 'weight loss' or 'increased energy'. The truth is that any fresh extra virgin olive oil has a whole host of benefits, but some companies spin it so that their particular oil seems 'better for you' than another. Of course, this could be the case if they have certified nutritional density and phenolic levels, but without proof, it's likely a scam.

Ignore

'FIRST COLD-PRESSED'
These days, this term is used purely for marketing purposes, as most modern and high-quality extra virgin olive is not actually pressed, it's extracted, and there is no second or third of anything – just one run and done for virgin oils. And cold? Relatively speaking, sure. EVOO is not heated up like refined oil, but produced at roughly room temperature (unless the label specifically states the temperature at which it has been processed). There are some producers who, due to the early time of year when they harvest and the prevailing heat in their region, take measures to keep the olives cool while being transported and to protect them from heat generated by mill equipment. But the word 'cold' as a descriptor of the extraction process typically means 'without added heat'.

OLIVE OIL COLOUR
Colour is not an indicator of quality. Yes, it is tempting to see a beautiful bright green oil and think it's better – but it's just patently not true. In fact, in olive oil competitions and during certifications, the colour is masked by azure blue tasting glasses so that opinions on quality are not influenced.

A Sommelier's Guide to Buying a Good EVOO

There's so much noise in the olive oil space. It's difficult to know what's liquid gold and what's just hype. If you're going to splash out on a nice bottle of olive oil, here's what to look out for on the label.

EXTRA VIRGIN

There are a few different oils that come from olives – and they're not all equal. If it doesn't say 'virgin', then it's refined and highly processed, losing the flavour and nutrition. Additionally, if it doesn't say 'extra', it's not the same high quality and will have defects – however small – even if it is made without heat over 27°C (80°F) or chemicals in a similar way.

HARVEST DATE

If the harvest date isn't obvious on the label, it's impossible to tell how fresh the oil is. Freshness is directly tied to flavour and nutrition, so without this information, you're blind. Olive oil is generally said to have a 'best before' date of two years from the date it's bottled if stored properly – away from light, heat and air – but we recommend less than 18 months from harvest for the best impact. Note: the expiry or 'best before' date legally only has to be from when it was bottled, which in the case of a commodity product like olive oil could be months or even a year after it was extracted in the mill.

PROVENANCE

Where, exactly, does this oil come from? Look for a precise region(s) of origin. Don't believe that just because it has an Italian name, it is 100 per cent made in Italy. There is nothing wrong with a blend, but a producer should be transparent about the region or regions the oil is sourced from if that's the case. If they can't narrow it down to a small area, it's a red flag about how they're running their supply chain and how removed they are from the 'first mile' of their olive oil (or, in this case, how little they know about the actual farmers making their product). It also says they're focused on volume, not quality.

VARIETIES

What types of olives are being used? The cultivar should be disclosed – 'Arbequina', for example – because it shows a connection to the land and a respect for the integrity of the end product. Much like different types of wine grapes or coffee beans, each variety of olive has its own distinct flavour – from green, peppery and vegetal all the way to mellow, grassy and floral. In addition, different varieties can each have a different shelf life. The information on a label therefore reveals if the producer has a genuine knowledge of the supply chain and cares about the product as a whole.

PRICE

Is the price fair? This is difficult to judge because so many things can affect the cost, but essentially EVOO should be priced well above refined oils, since it is a fresh, nutrient-rich product. Note too, the earlier the harvest in the season, the less oil can be extracted from the fruit, so the higher the price. Also, oils produced from traditional groves that go in for hand-harvesting and artisanal techniques involve more labour costs, and this is reflected in the selling price as well.

Many supermarkets are notorious for selling extra virgin olive oil at a price that is less than what it costs to produce. Strip back store margins, transport, bottling, labelling, testing, export – and you can start to see the base cost per litre. That is what will go to the producer, who then needs to account for milling, labour, energy and all the agricultural costs all year long for this one harvest. Remember, if an oil has a premium price but the details listed here are not all disclosed on the label – avoid it. You could be paying for pretty packaging and not much else.

SOME LABEL EXTRAS I LOVE TO SEE

ACIDITY

The free fatty acid level of extra virgin olive oil must, by IOC regulation, be under 0.8%. For a speciality oil, you're looking for under 0.3%, and for a top-quality oil, it can be under 0.2%. (Some of our producers regularly hit around 0.1%, which is absolute perfection and indicative of the intense focus on quality that has been exerted at every single step of the production journey.) This type of acidity can be determined only by chemical analysis, not by taste. So what's the point of this information in relation to the shopper? Basically, the lower the level of acidity, the more stable the oil will be for high-heat cooking, as well as having a better shelf life in general.

POLYPHENOLS

These are antioxidant compounds, and some that are celebrated for their anti-inflammatory properties are unique to virgin olive oils. By EU regulation, oils considered 'high polyphenol' must contain at least 250mg per kg, but I like to see a total number at least double that figure for a 'high' one. This is because polyphenols tend to drop by 40% over the year from harvest, so I want to ensure the content is still high even after the oil has naturally mellowed.

How to Taste Olive Oil

If you're going to spend the money required to get a real 'extra virgin', it's worth understanding what you're actually dealing with. Pop open that new bottle and let's explore what it has to offer.

To do this right, you should taste your olive oil when you first open the bottle. That's because EVOO should be used while fresh. This means as close to harvest as possible, ideally under 18 months unopened or within 2–3 months once opened. I'd also recommend washing your hands, especially if you're handling other ingredients in the kitchen, but steer clear of soaps with too much fragrance, as it'll throw you off.

At official tastings, a panel of judges would use small, stemless coloured glasses. The shape, much like a wine glass or a Glencairn whiskey glass, narrows towards the top in order to funnel the aromas upwards. The coloured glass, meanwhile, is to obscure the colour of the oil, so as to not let your eyes mislead you into thinking it's better or worse than it actually is.

1.

To start your own tasting, pour a shot of olive oil into a small dark glass. If you don't have such a thing, a wine glass or something similar will be fine. You need 15–20ml (3–4 teaspoons) of oil – enough to swirl around the glass and take a couple of sips.

2.

Cup the glass in one hand, then cover the top with your other hand. You're doing two things here: warming the oil up to body temperature, while also holding in the aromas. Try to bring it to something like your body temperature for 20–30 seconds.

3.

Now, here comes the magic. Remove your 'lid' hand and put your nose right in the glass, taking a deep breath in to bring those aromas now floating in the glass up into your smell receptors. For an even stronger hit, you can also cup your hands around your nose in the glass.

4.

Spin the glass and swirl some more, moving your nose side to side over the oil. (Did you know that one nostril often works better than the other? Find out which one in your case.) You can even open your mouth a bit – a trick I learned in a wine course.

Depending on the intensity of the oil, you might have already started to smell it the moment you poured it into the glass.

A medium-intensity oil might hit you at chin level, before you put your nose in the glass. A more delicate oil might take the full process to give you any sense of the aroma. That doesn't necessarily mean there's a problem. Softer, milder oils can be a thing of beauty. Subtle but nuanced, they can often elevate dishes in more ways than stronger oils, and allow other ingredients to shine without overpowering them.

5.

Think about what you smell. This is part one of identifying the key attributes of the oil.

FRUITINESS, as it's called in the olive oil world, doesn't refer simply to fruits. It's much more than that. I tell people to look for the smell of life. It should smell like plants – something living to represent that this is a fresh, living oil from a plant.

Common aromas in quality EVOO include fresh-cut grass or herbs, vegetables like artichoke or rocket, and fruits like tomatoes or apples. (Johnny Madge, one of my mentors and a legend in the olive oil world, enjoys the fact that we had the smell of tomatoes in some oils long before the fruit itself was introduced to Europe from the Americas.)

Common defects that you do not want to smell include wax or crayon, wine or vinegar, or anything chemical or metal.

6.

Now to taste. Cover the cup again with your hand and give it a swirl. Let's take a small sip, about a teaspoonful, but don't swallow just yet. Hold this right at the front of your mouth for a second to settle in and then aerate it, just as professionals would with wine or tea. To do this, open your mouth and, as our producer Marianna Devetzoglou recommends, 'Smile like a Cheshire cat!' Put your tongue to the roof of your mouth and take a few shallow breaths through the sides of your mouth, sucking in air and pushing the oil back along the sides of your tongue. The Italians have a word for this technique – stripaggio, which means 'stripping'. It's a way to evaluate the oil by letting it coat all of your taste buds and membranes with tiny droplets, triggering the right sensations to capture and identify all of the notes.

At this stage, you might be experiencing part two of what makes EVOO special...

BITTERNESS is a sensation that can range from a sharpness on the palate to something much slighter. It often gives oil a boldness or robustness that people associate with certain oils from Tuscany and southern Italy. An oil can also be mild, and that's OK too! Bitterness isn't required to be strong in an award-winning oil. But it is considered a positive attribute in EVOO, something that helps open up flavours and elevates the whole experience of eating – even if, on its own, it's not your cup of tea.

7.

Now swallow. The bitterness is probably more apparent at this stage, if it exists in the particular oil you are tasting. Unlike tasting wine or spirits, where you can spit, when tasting EVOO, the sensations after swallowing are an important part of the experience and quality detection, so you've got to go all in. You might cough at this point, and that's a totally normal reaction to some oils' properties. So let's talk about the final thing you're looking for.

PEPPERINESS, often called 'pungency', can provoke a little tingle in the back of the throat, or a full-on coughing fit, with a wasabi-like hit on the nose and a burning sensation on the lips. The strength of this reaction depends on several factors, including variety, harvest, production, the climate that year... But what pepperiness ultimately represents is one of the most magical elements in olive oil, one that exists only in virgin (unrefined) oils – oleocanthal. This special polyphenol compound is a strong antioxidant that, according to the US National Library of Medicine, 'shares unique perceptual and anti-inflammatory characteristics with ibuprofen'. It's extra special.

After you feel the pepper (or not), pause and get a feel for what's happening as you breathe out through your nose. This is when you'll have a 'retronasal experience', which is much more pleasant than it sounds. Swallowing taps into the retronasal olfactory route – essentially that connection between the nose and the mouth. The fragrance and flavour from the oil make their way to the back of your throat – the place where smell and taste come together. I often find that closing my mouth at this point and breathing out through my nose adds another layer to what I've just sensed.

Of the holy trinity of extra virgin olive oil – fruitiness, bitterness and pepperiness – the most celebrated factor is fruitiness, but having all three elements exist harmoniously in balance is what makes for a stand-out oil.

An oil that doesn't bring you any fruity gifts but just hits you with a pungent aftertaste isn't great. The same goes for something that's all bitterness and no fruit – it needs something nice on the nose. The balance of these qualities is what you should be looking for: in a delicate way to complement many different foods, or in a bolder way to give direction to a dish.

It starts with knowing what to look for and making sure you've got a keeper. Once you've found some oils you like, you can experiement to see which oils complement which dishes, and when to cook with what. It's not until you've smelled and sipped your EVOO on its own that you know if it's fresh, and how to use it. What do its aromas inspire you to make? That's what your oil should be telling you.

Common Defects

It's not all good stuff that you might find when you properly smell and taste olive oil. Having gone through the good things, it's important to know the qualities you do not want to encounter. Below are the main ones we look for in professional tastings.

DEFECT	CAUSE/SMELL	TASTE
Rancid	Oxidation, caused by contact with air, heat or light. The oil could also just be old.	Old nuts and frying oil, or old cosmetics.
Fusty	Fermentation (anaerobic) from keeping piled up olives (often in sacks) without oxygen.	Barnyard, wet hay or stables. Sometimes a smell like pickled olives, tapenade, or even baked pie, when the olives are grubby, poorly handled, or stored too long.
Muddy sediment	Often from unfiltered oils left with sediment for a long time, or from storage tanks that have not been properly cleaned.	Mud, swampy, sewage (oh, it gets worse...), vomit and roadkill.
Musty/mouldy fruit	Common with windfall olives collected off the ground, or from olives stored too long in a humid environment, where they have developed yeast.	Mouldy, earthy; damp potatoes or bread mould; cellar with wet dust.
Winey/vinegary	Aerobic fermentation after olives have been bruised, and left sitting in that state for too long before milling. Also from olive flies, which damage the fruit, or from using an old, unclean press.	As the name suggests, bad wine or vinegar. Sometimes nail polish remover or more like a solvent.
Stewed/burnt	Overheating while being milled.	A bit jammy, or like overcooked vegetables, old cooking oil, popcorn.
Grubby	Infestation by olive flies.	A slightly dirty, 'animal' smell. Slightly rancid notes with rotten fruit elements. 'Dirty' describes it spot on.
Frozen fruit/wet wood	Damage by frost.	Wet wood, such as an ice-cream stick or bamboo cutlery. Sometimes custard and stewed fruit.

SUBJECTIVITY

Note that many of the tasting notes – both good and bad – are somewhat subjective based on the aromas and flavours you're used to.

In some parts of the world, people have preferences for styles that the IOC and the official tasting panels would call 'defective'. For example, in places where it's not easy to access a good mill within a short period of time after harvesting, the quality of the oil will naturally be affected, leading to fermentation. The same goes for oils that aren't filtered and contain too much sediment.

I've broken bread and tasted oils with people from regions where, culturally, the flavours of what would be considered 'defective' oils are preferred. From a nutrition perspective, they don't hold up as well, but there are certainly worse things you could consume.

I can see from lab analysis that even olive oils with some light defects are still much healthier than their ultra-processed, refined shelf mates. And in the case of 'virgin' olive oils that have limited defects but are not good enough to be designated 'extra', any odd flavour typically disappears during heating, so they make for wonderful cooking oils – often with some decent antioxidants and at a lower price point than an extra virgin olive oil.

BLENDS: GOOD OR BAD?

To many people, the word 'blend' brings to mind bad oils, often involving mixing a dash of extra virgin into refined oils for a hint of flavour and authenticity. That's definitely a problem. However, 'blend' is also a term applied to a mix of extra virgin olive oils from different places or varieties. Some people prefer these, while others swear by a monocultivar (single variety). It's a similar argument that we find in the whiskey space about single malts or blends. Sometimes a blend can become better than the sum of its parts.

Blends become bad when they lack transparency and traceability, and are purely made for volume. They can be good when the different cultivars better support pollination or when they are specifically produced for a more flavourful or balanced profile. It's worth remembering that some of the world's greatest wines are blends, with Bordeaux (primarily made up of Merlot, Cabernet Sauvignon and Cabernet Franc) being probably the most famous. Similarly, Central Italian EVOOs from Tuscany and Umbria are classically made by blending Moraiolo, Frantoio and Leccino to get the depth and complexity those regions are famous for. Here's how we define oil blends:

Field blends: The most natural blend in olive oil, where different varieties are all pulled from the same grove or estate and milled together at the same time.

Blends of different batches from a single origin: This can happen on a small-scale level, where a single producer blends the different batches from their different cultivars. Like whiskey or wine, this is often about creating balance or a specific flavour profile.

Blends of different regions: Typically done for large-scale brands that need to make a consistent, singular profile, and need as much oil as they can get access to. It's not about characterful flavour or unique expression, and the taste of place is lost.

Blends of different oil types: This is no longer extra virgin, so it's important is to understand 100% of what the ingredients are. Sometimes the blend might be from just olives, but it could also be a blend of seed or nut oils.

Can You Cook with Olive Oil?

Let's set the record straight: you can and you should cook with olive oil. The belief that you shouldn't is a myth that desperately needs busting. The main concern seems to be about the 'smoke point' being too low, which is nonsense, as EVOO is perfectly suited to all your normal cooking temperatures. While some people think it's 'too good' to cook with, that goodness is what makes it the right choice, for the sake of your health and the quality of your home cooking.

The misconceptions surrounding cooking with EVOO have unjustly caused a generation to shy away from all its potential, and instead swap it for an industrial-grade, refined and 'lifeless' fat. So let me make an important point: virgin olive oil is a whole food, and has been safely consumed by people for thousands of years. The Mediterranean diet is celebrated as one of the healthiest in the world, with extra virgin olive oil as its primary fat and an indispensable ingredient for cooking. It's now high time to embrace the simplicity and quality of this foundational ingredient.

Some people claim to dislike EVOO because it has such a strong flavour, but I can firmly tell you that's only because they haven't experimented enough. There is such a wide variety of intensities and flavours in virgin oils that it really is possible to find something for everyone. Added to that, some of EVOO's key characteristics will 'cook off' when heat is applied, decreasing its flavour. It must be said that heating also removes some of the nutritional compounds that contribute so much to the oil, but those that do remain make it miles ahead of any of other oils you might reach for.

When I was younger, my grandfather, who was from a farming background, once explained to me what he ate in a day, going on about all the vegetables he ate and how he cooked everything with extra virgin. 'It's the only oil I use,' he told me. Having read articles about the notorious 'smoke point', I quickly jumped in to say he shouldn't be using EVOO, since 'something about heating it makes it carcinogenic'. He looked directly at me and said, 'Is that so?' And then kept on cooking with it into his nineties.

He was right to do so. Consistently debunked by science and medical bodies across the world, this dangerous falsehood, likely stirred up by the same people who tried to sell us on fat-free food and fake sugars, still lingers in our kitchens – even being spoken about to this day among the food community.

WHAT IS SMOKE POINT?
Let's start with a definition. Smoke point is the temperature threshold at which a cooking oil starts to give off visible smoke and undergo chemical breakdown. In terms of this, not all olive oils are created equal. Quality makes all the difference. Typically, extra virgin olive oil, which is high in polyphenols and low in acidity, holds up best to heating and has a smoke point of 190–220°C (375–425°F). Given this, it's time to stop worrying about smoke point because most

of what you do in the home kitchen is usually happening at under 200°C (400°F). Roasting tops out at 220°C (425°F), most baking happens under the 200°C (400°F) threshold, sautéing hits around 120°C (250°F), and deep-frying is usually within the range of 175–190°C (340–375°F). If, for some reason, you crank up the heat and reach the smoke point, your senses will alert you to it immediately – it's an unmistakable smell.

I don't recommend that you regularly fry or deep-fry your food, but if you do so at the right temperature, it will absorb less oil and make it a healthier option. So make sure to use a good oil that gives you something extra. (A 2015 study published in the *Journal of Food Chemistry* found that the phenols and antioxidants in extra virgin olive oil transfer to vegetables during the cooking process, thus increasing their nutritional content.)

Multiple studies now show that cooking with extra virgin olive oil not only makes food taste better, but also boosts the phytonutrients your body craves. Of course, the best way to get the nutrients is raw, but that doesn't mean you shouldn't use EVOO at every stage of your cooking. As our producer Dimitris in Crete says: 'Less in the pan, more on the plate.'

WHICH EVOO SHOULD YOU CHOOSE?

That all comes down to what you want it for. We need to think of olive oil more like wine when it comes to pairing. Not every bottle is going to suit everything.

I believe that all home cooks should equip themselves with a versatile trio of EVOOs:

1. THE DELICATE POUR
A finishing oil for those dishes you don't want to dominate, or cooler, fresher plates. Ideal for sauces, such as pesto and mayo, and for drizzling over salads and desserts.

2. THE INTENSE POUR
A bolder oil with punched-up peppery and bitter notes – great for warm, cosy plates. Perfect with more vibrant flavours, as well as with roasted veg, grilled meats, and cheese.

3. THE COOKING POUR
Probably a later-harvest oil with more mellow notes. It could even be a simple virgin olive oil, or one from the previous harvest. The point is that it's more economical than extra virgin. In my kitchen, the last remnants of old bottles go into a 'catch all' blend that I collect in a ceramic bottle. This is my first choice for frying or coating ingredients.

Work EVOO into Everything

Once you start to see how EVOO can transform even the most unexpected of foods and notice how your body responds over time, you'll want to pull away from refined oils that have zero flavour and nothing to offer nutritionally. There's no meal that EVOO can't improve, and it's categorically better for you.

BREAKFAST:
Use it to fluff up your smoothies, to drizzle on toast, and to fry your egg. It makes an omelette infinitely more nutritious, and it's great in banana bread and pancakes.

LUNCH:
Do what the Europeans do and make your own dressing. It's super easy, and it can be used across salads, sandwiches and for dips. Soups also benefit from a swirl across the top!

DINNER:
Fry and roast your veggies in olive oil. Marinade your meat in it for extra flavour and to give a perfect caramelized finish.

DESSERT:
Drizzle over chocolate and ice cream. Baking with extra virgin olive oil is also quite straightforward. Use 3 parts olive oil for every 4 parts butter, so 1 tablespoon oil instead of each 20g (¾oz) butter.

SETTING UP YOUR MEDITERRANEAN PANTRY

If you want to follow the Mediterranean diet and experience all the flavours and health benefits associated with it, then let's make sure you have everything you need on hand to do that with ease. The beauty and simplicity of it is simply a few fresh and seasonal ingredients, with a cupboard ready to go at any time for a quick meal.

Here's what that looks like, according to olive oil producers:

- Breadsticks and/or crackers
- Anchovies or other canned fish in oil
- Capers in brine
- Cheese for cooking (feta and Parmesan)
- Chocolate, dark
- Dried herbs and spices, such as oregano, paprika and cinnamon
- Dried or canned beans
- Fresh herbs (thyme, basil, parsley, mint)
- Garlic
- Honey
- Lemons, for zest and juice
- Nuts (walnuts or almonds)
- Olives in brine, at least two different kinds. I'm a fan of Castelvetrano/ Nocellara (big and buttery); Kalamata (rich and dark); Gordal (nice for stuffing)
- Pasta
- Raisins and/or sultanas
- Sea salt
- Short-grain rice, such as Bomba or Arborio
- Sun-dried tomatoes
- Tomatoes, chopped and canned
- Tomato passata
- Tomato purée
- Tomato sauce, homemade from summer produce, or good-quality ready-made sauce
- Vinegar
- Wine, for drinking and cooking
- Yogurt, plain Greek-style

Oil you need to know...

Keeping this book concise and focussing on the recipes has been no easy task. EVOO is a topic I feel deeply passionate about. It's an obsession. Falling in love with olive oil felt like diving into the world of wine – only somehow even more romantic, more natural and certainly more spiritual. But if you read nothing else and just want the key points without any of the lyrical waxing about liquid gold from an eternal tree, then here they are.

Buy Better

Look out for the key indicators of quality: harvest date, varieties, where it comes from and how it's packaged up.

H.A.L.T

The enemies of extra virgin olive oil are heat, air, light and time. Store it away from the stove and in an airtight container that blocks out light. Use within 18 months of harvest, or within 3 months of opening.

Don't Save it – Savour it

EVOO is to pour rather than store. It doesn't get better with age; it's at its healthiest and most vibrant soon after harvest.

Elevate Everything

Use it daily however you want. Drizzle, dip, glug, pour, cook and fry. This is a transformative ingredient for your food and your health.

Breakfast

'There isn't a meal I don't
have olive oil with.'

—Nick Wilkinson, Rio Largo Olive Estate, Breede River Valley, South Africa

Chocolate & EVOO on Toast

This recipe is our take on a Catalan classic. In my 20s, I was living in Spain and giving English classes. This little after-school treat always brought joy, and first introduced me to the many interesting ways you can use olive oil, but it was El Bulli's Ferran Adrià who put this basic snack on the culinary stage. Simple, and yet surprisingly indulgent. Here, we jazz it up slightly with a little heat.

Serves 4

- 100g (3½oz) plain dark chocolate (60% cocoa solids)
- 4 slices of your favourite bread
- 2–4 tablespoons EVOO
- ½–1 teaspoon sea salt flakes
- pinch of ground cinnamon

Preheat the grill, or heat a griddle pan over a medium–high heat. (Toast tastes nicer when made this way, but you can use a toaster if you're feeling lazy.)

Coarsely grate the chocolate onto a plate.

Toast the bread until golden on both sides by whichever method you prefer.

Place it on plates and spoon the grated chocolate over the top – it will start to melt immediately. Drizzle with the olive oil, then sprinkle with the salt and cinnamon and serve straight away.

MAKE IT YOUR OWN
Add a teaspoon of cocoa nibs or chilli flakes to the melted chocolate. Some finely grated orange zest also makes it extra special.

EVOO TO PAIR
For a gentle contrast, choose Arbequina, Leccino, Megaritiki or Manaki. For a marked contrast, and to play up the bitter notes from the chocolate, try a Croatian oil from Istria.

Matcha EVOO

When the trend for putting olive oil in coffee kicked off a few years ago (and entered the mainstream via Starbucks), we were super-keen to find out more. We started testing different styles and formats, and learned a few things along the way. Among these was how beautiful a good olive oil could be in matcha – perhaps even better than it is in coffee – thanks to the inherent plant flavours you find in this style of green tea. This recipe comes to us from our producer Lena in Croatia, who makes this as her morning brew. You can also try it on a visit to her tasting room at Brist Olive Oil in Istria.

Serves 1

- 1 teaspoon ceremonial grade matcha tea powder
- 1 teaspoon honey or maple syrup
- 1 teaspoon extra virgin olive oil
- 250ml (9fl oz) milk of your choice

Put the matcha powder and your sweetener of choice into a teacup. Add 1 tablespoon freshly boiled water and whisk to a thick paste. If you have a special bamboo matcha whisk so much the better.

While still whisking, add the EVOO and continue whisking until smooth.

Heat the milk until steaming, then use a handheld milk frother or small whisk to whizz the hot milk until foamy.

Add the frothed milk to the matcha and serve immediately.

EVOO TO PAIR
Grassy notes work well here, so Leccino, Koroneiki and Buža (from Croatia) are good choices.

Olive Oil Scones

The Portuguese do pastries very well, but this is a Mediterranean spin on a uniquely English bake. Using olive oil intead of butter is just the sort of 'swap' you can make when exploring baking with EVOO. This recipe comes to us from our producer Ana Cardoso of Tratturo de Fronteira in Alentejo: 'A recipe I found a few years ago and have used ever since. A real challenge to the English version, but well worth a try!' These scones are lovely with the Olive Oil Chantilly (see page 171) or simply with jam or EVOO-roasted strawberries.

Makes 8

- 200g (7oz) plain flour
- 8g (1½ teaspoons) baking powder
- pinch of salt
- 30g (1oz) caster sugar
- 2 tablespoons extra virgin olive oil
- 125ml (4fl oz) whole milk

Preheat the oven to 200°C (180°C fan/400°F/Gas mark 6) and line a baking tray with nonstick baking paper.

Sift the flour, baking powder and salt into a bowl. Add the sugar and mix to combine.

Add the olive oil and milk and mix using a palette knife or table knife, but do not overwork the dough; it should just come together and doesn't need to be smooth and thoroughly combined.

Using 2 spoons, divide the dough into 8 equal pieces and place on the prepared tray, spacing them slightly apart. There's no need for rolling out or to make smooth balls – these scones are free-form.

Bake for 20–25 minutes, or until golden.

MAKE IT YOUR OWN
Adding raisins or chocolate chips to the mixture is always a good idea.

TIP
The scones are best eaten fresh from the oven, but should you want to do some in bulk, you can freeze the dough pieces and bake them directly from frozen.

EVOO TO PAIR
Something fruity, such as Galega, Arbequina, Taggiasca or Biancolilla.

Lemon & EVOO Elixir

This drink started a TikTok trend – one we were quite surprised by as a team – but the ingredients themselves are solid from a nutritional standpoint. In fact, it's now become our recommended prescription when a member of the team is feeling run down or when the London winter takes its toll on our immune systems.

Serves 2-4

- 1 organic unwaxed lemon, roughly quartered
- 2cm (¾in) piece of fresh root ginger, peeled and roughly chopped
- 2 tablespoons extra virgin olive oil
- 2 tablespoons raw honey
- 700ml (1¼ pints) water

Place all the ingredients in a blender and blitz at high speed until thoroughly combined. The mixture should be slushy and pale yellow.

Strain through a sieve into a jug, pressing on the pulp with the back of a spoon to extract as much goodness as possible. Pour into small glasses and drink!

MAKE IT YOUR OWN
If you want to jazz up this drink, add some mint or basil, and it's practically a mocktail. Or lean into those 'start your morning right' flavours with an added shot of apple cider vinegar.
You could also try adding a little turmeric – either peeled fresh root or powdered – and a twist of black pepper.
My mother skips the ginger, but adds lime juice and chives as a part of a holistic morning routine to keep her blood pressure in check.

TIP
Fresh is best – this drink is most enjoyable with the froth that forms in the blender.

EVOO TO PAIR
Choose an early-harvest oil for its higher polyphenol content.

Breakfast Smoothie

Inspired by our producer Nick Wilkinson from Rio Largo in South Africa, whose health transformation led him on a journey to becoming an olive oil farmer and miller, this is the smoothie that Citizens of Soil co-founder Michael Vachon makes a version of every morning. Adding EVOO means you not only get the benefit of its healthy fats to help kick-start your day, but it also gives the smoothie a fluffier, creamier texture. It actually creates the same effect as barista-style plant milks, which contain added seed oils for creaminess – but this is doing it in a more natural, healthy way.

Serves 1

- 60g (2¼oz) frozen berries of choice
- ½ banana, fresh or frozen
- 300ml (½ pint) almond or cashew milk
- 30g (1oz) protein powder of your choice
- 2 tablespoons extra virgin olive oil

OPTIONAL EXTRAS

- ½ teaspoon vanilla extract
- 1–3 teaspoons smooth peanut butter, for extra flavour and higher fat content

Tip all the ingredients into a high-speed blender and blitz until smooth. Pour into a tall glass and drink right away.

MAKE IT YOUR OWN
Try adding greens, such as spirulina powder or even fresh kale. Swap flavours according to the season.

TIPS
You can use fresh fruit if it's in season, but then you'll need to add a few ice cubes to cool the smoothie and make it the right consistency.
Be sure to use a plant-based milk without any added oils. Many barista versions include refined oils, which don't work in this recipe.

EVOO TO PAIR
Greek oils of medium intensity work nicely here.

Tuscan Beans in Broth on Garlic Toast

Everyone in the olive oil world has their go-to recipe when the new-harvest oils arrive, and this is the one from Tuscany. Their bitter and pungent green oils so early in the harvest season really make this dish. Our producers Candice and Fabrizio from Olea Prilis sent us this recipe for a hearty snack, ideal as the weather cools, and a great way of trying their oils. Once assembled, you will have created the typical Tuscan 'bruschetta', second only to 'fett'unta', which is simply grilled bread drizzled with new-harvest oil.

Serves 6

- **250g (9oz) dried cannellini beans or, if you can find them, Pratomagno Zolfini Beans from Tuscany – a dream!**
- **1 teaspoon bicarbonate of soda**
- **1 large sprig of sage**
- **1 whole head of garlic**
- **sea salt flakes and freshly ground black pepper**

TO SERVE

- **4 thick slices of sourdough bread**
- **2 garlic cloves**
- **extra virgin olive oil**

TIP
Warning from the Tuscans: it's absolutely forbidden to add cheese to this recipe!

EVOO TO PAIR
Tuscan varieties, such as Frantoio and Moraiolo, as well as Coratina from Southern Italy. An early-harvest Greek oil, such as Kalamon or Koroneiki, can be beautiful.

Start by soaking the beans in a large bowl of cold water with the bicarbonate soda for about 6 hours, or overnight.

Drain the beans through a colander and wash them thoroughly under cold running water. Transfer to a large saucepan and cover them with 4 times their depth of fresh water. Add the sage and garlic, and bring to the boil over a medium heat.

Once boiling, lower the heat and cook the beans at a gentle simmer for about 1 hour, until al dente. Use a slotted spoon to remove any scum that rises to the surface.

Add a generous pinch of salt and continue cooking for a further 15–30 minutes, or until the beans are tender.

Meanwhile, toast or grill the bread until crisp and golden brown. Rub each slice with raw garlic and place in bowls or on deep plates.

Pour over about 3 tablespoons of the boiled beans and half a ladleful of the cooking broth. Season with sea salt flakes and pepper, and drizzle with a generous slick of olive oil to serve.

If stored in a lidded container, cooked beans will keep for 2–3 days in the fridge.

Tapas & Aperitivos

'Our olive oil and the cultivation of our trees is our way to connect with the land, the Earth, our ancestors, and each one of our customers.'

—Christina Chrisoila, Taxidi Olive Farm, Crete, Greece

The 50/50 Olive Oil Martini

When we first launched Citizens of Soil, the olive oil martini became the serve we got tagged in the most on Instagram. Now we do limited-edition drops of olive oil vodka with 'Cocktail Carmen' of 58 and CO distillery and masterclasses to explore how different olive oil profiles can change this drink. This 'wet' version, which goes lighter on the booze and more in on the flavour, is a winner. It's best garnished with a chunky olive and served with a gilda, like in the photo on page 45. Gildas are the first tapa I order at any bar in Spain: this classic Basque pintxo often consists of a Manzanilla or Gordal olive, anchovy filet and a guindilla pepper on a skewer, finished with a drizzle of EVOO. Fat, acid, salt, drink! A dream pairing.

Makes 1

- **40ml (2½ tablespoons) dry white vermouth**
- **40ml (2½ tablespoons) vodka or gin**
- **handful of ice cubes**
- **½ teaspoon extra virgin olive oil**
- **twist of lemon peel or a Nocellara green olive (or why not both?)**

Add the vermouth and vodka to a cocktail mixing glass with the ice cubes and stir until the martini is ice cold.

Strain into a chilled coupe glass and drizzle a few drops of EVOO on top.

Finish with a twist of lemon peel or a green olive and drink immediately.

MAKE IT YOUR OWN
You can obviously dial the ratio of spirits up or down. For a dry martini, you'd traditionally have around 60ml (4 tablespoons) of the spirit and just 5ml (1 teaspoon) of the vermouth in the mix, so find your right split. This version is about taking the edge off a strong drink while still enjoying the punchy savouriness it offers.

TIP
Place some coupes or martini glasses in the freezer ahead of time so that the martini stays cooler and fresher for longer once poured into the glass.

EVOO TO PAIR
Choose an early-harvest oil that will give an extra peppery kick. Nocellara would be great here, but also something such as an Hojiblanca or Koroneiki.

Olive Oil Spritz Cocktail

The spritz is rooted in northern Italy, going back more than a century, when soldiers from the occupying Austro–Hungarian empire liked to add water to the local wine. Since then, it has come to mean a cocktail based on a bitter liqueur, such as Aperol, Campari or Cynar, that is mixed with sparkling wine. The home of the Aperol spritz is Venice, where in the backstreet bacaris (wine bars) you will be asked if you want it 'internazionale' (with prosecco) or Veneziano (made with local white wine). Here we have a recipe from the lovely Kate Carruthers, who's a food writer and recipe developer, most notably with the Ottolenghi team. She helped us nail the ratios when we wanted a little EVOO to spruce up our summer spritz. It really gives a full-palate experience.

Makes 1

- **2 handfuls of ice cubes**
- **50ml (2fl oz) Aperol**
- **1 teaspoon olive brine**
- **½ teaspoon extra virgin olive oil**
- **75ml (2½fl oz) prosecco**
- **dash of soda water**
- **slice of orange**
- **3–4 green olives**

Pop a handful of ice cubes into a cocktail mixing glass, add the Aperol, olive brine and EVOO and stir with some speed.

Strain into a large wine glass and add the prosecco, soda water and a fresh handful of ice.

Garnish with a slice of orange and the olives. Eating the Aperol-marinated olives at the end is almost as good as the spritz itself.

MAKE IT YOUR OWN
Feel free to play around with the aperitivo base. Campari or Cynar are stronger than Aperol, but taste great too. When it comes to bubbles, stick with a good-quality prosecco – there's no need to waste a fine champagne. But whatever fizz you choose, make sure it's dry, freshly opened and served fast.

TIP
Always add the final amount of ice at the end of the process, just before you garnish.

EVOO TO PAIR
Let's go Venetian and try Grignano. Go more mellow with a Leccino or more intense with Coratina or Frantoio.

Cretan Dakos

Think simple Italian bruschetta or Spanish pan con tomate, but heartier and with more tang. Called a 'salad' on menus in Greece, this Cretan dish is a staple and exactly the sort of thing you can easily whip up for a satisfying snack. Traditionally made with old barley bread, these paximadi (literally 'rusks') are brought to life with juicy ripe tomatoes, crumbled feta and lashings of EVOO. The result is a combination of crunchy, salty, creamy – decidedly Greek – flavours.

Serves 4–6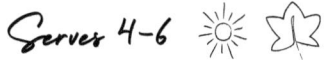

- 4 large barley rusks, or thick slices of stale, dense bread
- 2–3 ripe tomatoes, finely chopped
- handful of pitted black olives, roughly chopped
- 1 tablespoon capers (optional)
- ½ red onion, thinly sliced (optional)
- ½–1 teaspoon dried oregano
- 100–150g (3½–5½oz) feta or mizithra cheese
- 100ml (3½fl oz) extra virgin olive oil
- sea salt flakes

If using traditional Greek rusks, lightly sprinkle them with water to soften just slightly, but they should still have crunch.

Mix the tomatoes and olives together in a bowl. Add the capers and onion (if using), and season with sea salt flakes and a generous dusting of oregano.

Place the rusks or bread on small plates or a serving tray. Spoon the chopped tomato and olive mixture evenly over the top.

Crumble the cheese over each piece and drizzle with extra virgin olive oil – don't hold back!

Serve immediately while the bread is still crisp on the bottom and juicy on top.

MAKE IT YOUR OWN

Use the pan con tomate technique and rub a garlic clove across the bread before assembling. Adding fresh herbs, such as basil, will make these dakos feel more Italian than Greek, while adding some anchovies will make them reminiscent of Spanish pintxo.

TIPS

This is a great way to use up old bread, but if you have only fresh bread, it can be toasted or grilled for the same effect.
If tomatoes aren't in season, try adding some vinegar or lemon juice to the olive oil and olives to make a nice dressing. Spoon this onto the bread, with the feta and dried oregano on top.

EVOO TO PAIR

Koroneiki or Tsounati – anything robust and fruity that sings with fresh tomato and salty cheese.

Classic Cretan Lentils

Is there anything healthier and heartier than a big bowl of lentils? I'm a real fan of warming dhals, protein-packed lentil salads and, of course, the Mediterranean versions stewed with tomatoes and herbs. When I first went to study in Spain during my university years, my host madre must have made lentils for lunch every day, and I never got tired of them. Years later, when Maria, our producer in Crete, first put this lentil dish in front of me, all those lovely memories came flooding back. This dish offers cheap and cheerful nutrition to get us through any season.

Serves 4–6

- **250g (9oz) dried green lentils**
- **1 large onion**
- **2–3 sun-dried tomatoes**
- **2–3 fresh tomatoes**
- **3 tablespoons extra virgin olive oil, plus extra to serve**
- **1 garlic clove, crushed (optional)**
- **2 bay leaves**
- **good pinch of dried oregano**
- **splash of white wine or apple cider vinegar**
- **salt and freshly ground black pepper**

MAKE IT YOUR OWN
Adding chopped sweet peppers or chillies with the tomatoes will bring out an extra depth of flavour.

TIPS
This is a great dish for making ahead. Eat it hot as a soup, or leave the lentils to cool down, drain off some of the liquid and serve them in a salad. The Greeks are more mindful than most about what the seasons mean in terms of flavour and nutrients, so Maria says: 'It's best to grate a supply of tomatoes during the summer and store them in the freezer.'

Rinse the lentils under cold running water, then tip them into a pan. Cover with cold water and bring to the boil. Simmer for about 8 minutes, until just al dente.

Meanwhile, finely chop the onion and sun-dried tomatoes. Coarsely grate the fresh tomatoes using a box grater.

When the lentils are ready, Maria advises draining and rinsing them, 'otherwise the food will be a little brownish'.

Pour the olive oil into the empty lentil pan, add the onion and soften over a medium heat for about 7 minutes. Add the garlic, if using, and cook for a further minute.

Return the lentils to the pan, add all the prepared tomatoes, plus the bay leaves and oregano. Pour in just enough water to cover the lentils. 'The more water you add,' says Maria, 'the more the finished dish will look like a soup. Don't overdo it, though.'

Season with salt and pepper, stir to combine, and cook over a medium heat for a further 8–10 minutes, until the lentils are tender.

Add a splash of vinegar to taste, then serve with a generous swirl of EVOO.

EVOO TO PAIR
Koroneiki, Hojiblanca, or even something like a Coratina for a touch of pepper.

Taramasalata

Salata is Greek for salad, but in typical Greek form, this is more of a dip than what you'd imagine a salad to be. Made from fish roe, taramasalata is just a super simple punch of flavour to dip anything into – particularly in that dark end-of-winter season. 'We make this between February and March,' explains Marianna Devetzoglou of Oleosophia, our producer near Corinithia, 'mostly when we celebrate Clean Monday [the first day of Lent], which is also a day when we fly kites in Greece, so all around a day kids would look forward to.' This is ideal in a mezze platter with other dips and small bites.

Serves 4–5

- 2 slices of day-old white bread, preferably sourdough, crusts removed and cut into cubes
- 100g (3½oz) tarama (fish roe)
- 250ml (9fl oz) extra virgin olive oil, plus extra to serve
- juice from 1½ lemons
- 125ml (4fl oz) cold water

TO GARNISH
- parsley
- olives

Combine the cubed bread, tarama, EVOO and lemon juice in a blender. Blitz at a medium speed, slowly adding the water until the mixture is smooth.

Spoon into a bowl and garnish with parsley, olives and a drizzle of EVOO.

Serve with crisps, crackers or crudités.

MAKE IT YOUR OWN
Build up flavours with capers, dill and onion.

TIP
You can also use taramasalata as a spread in a sandwich.

EVOO TO PAIR
Manaiki for a more delicate taste or Koroneiki for something that will hold up to the flavours.

Trio of Cupboard Meze

This trio of recipes was inspired by our team 'golden hour' aperitivos that we started doing once a week in celebration of long summer days. Fern Speakman, a chef on our team, brought in two of these recipes and they were such a hit – simple, vegan and made mostly from things you could have sitting in your pantry. They, in turn, inspired a trio of Levantine flavours for a meze that's useful when fresh ingredients are lacking, but also great in the height of summer's vibrant bounty, when you just want to make something that doesn't require heat.

Each meze serves 4–6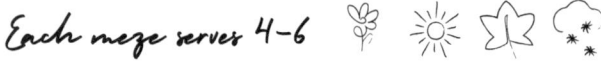

1. Roasted Pepper Muhammara

- 100g (3½oz) walnuts
- 360g (12½oz) roasted red peppers from a jar, drained
- 1 garlic clove, roughly chopped
- juice of 1 lemon
- ½ teaspoon ground cumin
- ½ teaspoon Aleppo pepper or chilli flakes, plus extra to serve
- ½ teaspoon sumac
- 1 teaspoon pomegranate molasses
- 3 tablespoons extra virgin olive oil, plus extra to serve
- 30–50g (1–1¾oz) panko breadcrumbs
- salt and freshly ground black pepper

Toast the walnuts in a dry frying pan over a medium heat, shaking them every few seconds so as not to burn. Set a few nuts aside for the topping and tip the rest into a blender or food processor.

Pat the roasted peppers dry on kitchen paper, then add to the blender with the remaining ingredients, adding just 30g (1oz) of the breadcrumbs to start with. Blend until smooth, adding more panko if needed to thicken. Season to taste.

Spoon into a bowl and top with some extra chilli flakes, the reserved toasted walnuts and a final drizzle of EVOO.

MAKE IT YOUR OWN
If you don't have pomegranate molasses, you could use date syrup, or even apricot jam at a push.

TIPS
Too sweet? Add some more lemon juice, spices or brine from the roasted red pepper jar for more tang.
Too spicy? Add some more breadcrumbs and lemon juice.
Too bland? Adjust the spices, salt and EVOO levels.

EVOO TO PAIR
Choose a bold Hojiblanca or Picual for richness, or go with a spicy Coratina to turn up the heat.

2. Artichoke Hummus

- 400g (14oz) can or jar chickpeas, drained, but liquid reserved
- 6 marinated artichoke hearts from a jar
- finely grated zest and juice of 1 unwaxed lemon
- 1 garlic clove, roughly chopped
- 1 tablespoon tahini
- 3 tablespoons extra virgin olive oil, plus extra to serve
- pinch of ground cumin
- 1 small ice cube
- salt and freshly ground black pepper

Tip the chickpeas, 4 of the artichokes, the lemon zest and half the juice into a blender or food processor, then add the garlic, tahini, EVOO and cumin. Season with salt and pepper and blend until smooth. Add a little of the chickpea water if needed to create a smooth, loose consistency. Season to taste with more lemon, cumin or salt.

Once the mixture is to your liking, add the ice cube and blend again. This will allow the oil to emulsify, making for a creamy and smoother consistency.

Spoon into a bowl and top with extra EVOO and the remaining artichoke hearts, quartered.

EVOO TO PAIR
The two dips on this page go best with medium to intense oils. Look for options like Picual, Frantoio, Hojiblanca, Kalamon or Koroneiki.

3. Harissa Bean Dip

- 400g (14oz) can butter beans, drained, but reserving 2–3 tablespoons of the liquid
- 1 fat garlic clove, roughly chopped
- 1 teaspoon ground cumin
- ½ teaspoon sweet paprika, plus extra to serve
- juice of ½ lemon
- 3 tablespoons extra virgin olive oil, plus extra to serve
- 1 tablespoon harissa or more to taste
- few fresh mint leaves or ½ teaspoon dried mint, plus extra to serve
- salt and black pepper

Put all the ingredients into a blender or food processor and blitz until smooth. Add a little of the reserved bean liquid if needed to loosen. Taste and add more spices, lemon, harissa or salt, as needed.

Spoon the dip into a serving bowl or dish and tear over the extra mint leaves, then sprinkle with paprika and more pepper. Drizzle over the extra EVOO to serve.

MAKE IT YOUR OWN
You could make this dip with other types of bean. Broad beans, for example, would make it the classic Moroccan dish bessara, especially with more fresh mint and thinly sliced red onion on top.

Mana'eesh Flatbread

An iconic Palestinian bread, mana'eesh is topped with a mixture of za'atar and olive oil. It is traditionally served hot from the oven, with chopped tomatoes, cucumber and labneh, and is a perfect more-ish snack. This recipe comes from Awad Melhim, an olive oil producer from Anin village in the Jenin district of Palestine. Our friends at Zaytoun, a British social enterprise that sources beautiful Palestinian products direct, kindly shared this recipe from him.

Makes 10

- **400g (14oz) strong white flour, plus extra for dusting**
- **2 teaspoons fast-action dried yeast**
- **1 teaspoon salt**
- **1 teaspoon caster sugar**
- **250ml (9fl oz) warm water**
- **100ml (3½fl oz) extra virgin olive oil**
- **2–3 tablespoons za'atar**
- **65g (2¼oz) finely grated cheese, such as Pecorino (optional)**

TO SERVE
- **sliced cucumbers and tomatoes**
- **labneh**

MAKE IT YOUR OWN
Chillies, feta or even a drizzle of hot honey all create something very nice!

TIP
You can make the dough in advance and freeze it, but the flatbread needs to be served freshly baked.

EVOO TO PAIR
A Palestinian variety, such as Nabali, Rumi or Souri, is the obvious choice. If those aren't available, Nocellara or Tonda Iblea from Sicily, or Greek Koroneiki would be lovely too.

Place the flour, yeast, salt and sugar in a large bowl and stir to combine. Add the warm water and 2 tablespoons EVOO and mix with a wooden spoon until a shaggy dough forms. Use your hands to bring the dough together, adding a little more water if it feels dry.

Turn the dough onto a work surface and knead for about 5 minutes, until smooth. Shape into a ball, return to the bowl, then cover with a tea towel and leave at room temperature for about 45 minutes, or until doubled in size.

Preheat the oven to 220°C (200°C fan/425°F/Gas mark 7) and line 2 baking sheets with nonstick baking paper.

Turn the dough onto a lightly floured work surface and divide into 10 equal pieces (about 70g/2½oz each). Roll each piece into a ball, then flatten in a circle 15–20cm (6–8in) wide.

You will most likely need to bake the flatbreads in batches, so place 2–4 circles on each prepared sheet, depending how many will neatly fit.

Brush the top of each circle with EVOO and sprinkle with za'atar, leaving the edges clear. Sprinkle with grated cheese, if you wish. Prick each circle a few times with a fork to prevent the dough from rising too much as it bakes.

Bake in batches for about 10 minutes, until puffy and golden. Wrap in a clean tea towel to keep warm while you bake the remaining flatbreads.

Serve warm as they are, or with labneh and sliced or chopped tomatoes and cucumber.

Roasted Grapes Crostini

So sweet, so jammy, so simple...roasted grapes are an easy way to jazz up a salad or cheese board. While the main focus of vineyards during the autumn may be on harvesting grapes for wine making, there will also be a beautiful range of snacking grapes in your local shops. This sweet and savoury combination, which highlights the shared spaces of vines and groves, is an easy, elegant thing to put on many dishes at this time of year.

Serves 4

- 1 bunch of sweet black grapes. about 500g (1lb 2oz)
- 1 sprig of rosemary or thyme
- 2–3 tablespoons extra virgin olive oil, plus extra to serve
- dash of balsamic vinegar
- 1 baguette or ciabatta loaf
- 1 garlic clove
- Gorgonzola, Fontina or a good goats' cheese
- salt and freshly ground black pepper

Preheat the oven to 210°C (190°C fan/410°F/Gas mark 6½).

Separate the grapes into small bunches and place them and the herbs on a baking tray. Drizzle with the EVOO and balsamic vinegar, then season with salt and pepper. Roast the grapes for 20–25 minutes, until they are soft and juicy.

Meanwhile, preheat the grill or a ridged griddle pan. Thinly slice the bread and toast each side using your preferred method.

Rub the garlic over the top of each slice of toast and sprinkle with the cheese. Top with a spoonful of the roasted grapes, pulled from the stem, then drizzle with the roasting juices and extra EVOO. Serve immediately.

MAKE IT YOUR OWN
Place a thin slice of prosciutto or coppa on the bread before adding the cheese.
You can also serve the roasted grapes with Greek yogurt or ice cream for a fully sweet treat.

TIP
You can roast the grapes ahead of time and store them in an airtight container for a couple of days, ready to spoon out when it's time to host.

EVOO TO PAIR
I prefer to use an oil with more bitter and green notes, like those from Tuscany and Istria.

Olives al Forno
Two Ways

The original version of this dish is made with fresh olives at harvest season, but a version using three different kinds of brined olives can be made all year round. Option 1 comes from Ana Cardoso, our producer in Portugal: 'The preparation of this appetizer varies greatly between friends and family. Some suggest leaving the olives in salt for a few days before preparing them, while others suggest boiling them. The most important thing is that the olives selected are healthy and ripe, black, but not soft.' If you happen to be near a decently yielding olive tree at the right time of year, you can try Option 2, a recipe from a recipe from Ana's husband, Paolo.

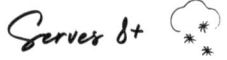 *Serves 8+*

1. Brined Olives al Forno

- 180g (6¼oz) brined black olives, such as Cerignola, rinsed
- 180g (6¼oz) brined green olives, such as Castelvetrano, rinsed
- 180g (6¼oz) brined olives, such as Kalamata, rinsed
- 100ml (3½fl oz) extra virgin olive oil
- 3 garlic cloves, sliced
- 1 unwaxed lemon, zest pared into strips
- 1 orange, washed and zest pared into strips
- 2 sprigs of thyme
- 2 bay leaves

Preheat the oven to 220°C (200°C fan/425°F/Gas mark 7).

Place all the ingredients in a large bowl and stir to combine. Pour into a shallow, ovenproof dish and place in the oven for 10–12 minutes, until bubbling.

Serve warm from the dish.

MAKE IT YOUR OWN
Add a sprig of fresh rosemary or a sliced preserved lemon.
If you like spice, chillies – fresh or dried –are a great addition. Or try adding spices such as coriander or cumin seeds, or a good pinch of dried oregano.

TIPS
The types of olive used can be whatever suits you, so long as they are different sizes, shapes and maturation (colours).
Don't let the olives overcook and change colour too much or they can become bitter.

EVOO TO PAIR
Try to pair to the olive type or the region, for example Kalemon or Nocellara.

2. Fresh Olives al Forno

- 175–250g (7–9oz) ripe olives from the tree
- 3–4 tablespoons extra virgin olive oil
- salt

Preheat the oven to 140°C (fan 120°C/275°F/Gas mark 1). Line a baking tray with baking paper.

Place the olives on the prepared tray, then season with salt and drizzle with the EVOO. Roast for about 5 hours, checking and turning the olives from time to time so that they cook and season evenly.

Set aside to cool, then season to taste and serve as an appetizer, or as a garnish for stews, braises and roasts.

Aubergine Fritters

Polpette di Melanzane

A classic example of cucina povera (peasant cooking), this dish is comforting, cheap and cheerful. The recipe comes to us from an English–Sicilian family, with groves in the province of Enna, bang in the middle of the island. Sarah Wolferstan and Paolo Guarino are micro-farmers in the village of Villarosa, splitting their time between their groves in Sicily and life back in Malmesbury, Wiltshire.

Serves 4

- **3 regular aubergines, or 2 large Sicilian ones**
- **100–125g (3½–4½oz) fresh breadcrumbs**
- **50g (1¾oz) Pecorino cheese, grated**
- **leaves from 3 sprigs of mint, finely chopped, plus extra to serve**
- **handful of flat leaf parsley, leaves finely chopped, plus extra to serve**
- **1 garlic clove, crushed**
- **2 eggs, lightly beaten**
- **3 tablespoons extra virgin olive oil**
- **salt and freshly ground black pepper**

Preheat the oven to 200°C (180°C fan/400°F/Gas mark 6).

Using a sharp knife, score the skin of each aubergine 4–5 times. Place them in a roasting tray and roast for about 40 minutes, until the flesh inside is soft. Set aside until cool enough to handle, then cut them in half and scoop the flesh into a sieve set over a bowl. Leave to drain for at least 2 hours, or even overnight.

Roughly chop the aubergine flesh and tip into a bowl. Add 100g (3½oz) of the breadcrumbs, the Pecorino, chopped herbs, garlic and eggs. Season with salt and pepper and mix to combine. The mixture should be dense enough for a small ball of it to hold its shape, so add more breadcrumbs if needed to bind the mixture together.

Shape the mixture into walnut-sized balls, then heat the olive oil in a frying pan. Add the polpette in batches and cook until crisp and golden on all sides.

Serve sprinkled with some extra parsley and mint.

TIP
The aubergines, or even the whole mixture, can be prepped a day in advance and stored in the fridge before frying; the polpette can also be frozen and defrosted as needed.

MAKE IT YOUR OWN
This is the sort of dish where you can sneak in some extra veg – chopped spinach or kale, grated carrots or courgettes – or extra protein in the form of cooked lentils or chickpeas.
Adding a little ricotta cheese to the mix will give the polpette creaminess.

EVOO TO PAIR
Opt for varieties of the region, such as Biancolilla, Cerasuola, Nocellara del Belice or Picual.

Cacio e Pepe Popcorn

When I first tried the EVOO from Ana in Alentejo, its early harvest notes were just so beautifully peppery and almost lemony sharp that all I wanted to do was put it over some cacio e pepe pasta. That sauce, in any way, is still a nice pairing for the oil Ana produces, but this combination was inspired by a friend telling me that she used nutritional yeast as a popcorn seasoning. After playing with these sharp-salty flavour combinations on corn on the cob, a snackable version was the natural next step.

Serves 4

- **4 tablespoons extra virgin olive oil**
- **100g (3½oz) popcorn kernels**
- **25g (1oz) Pecorino Romano or Parmesan cheese, or nutritional yeast to make it vegan**
- **salt and freshly ground black pepper**

MAKE IT YOUR OWN
Add some lemon zest to provide an acidic contrast to the savouriness. You could also add a pinch of chilli powder or smoked paprika for a hit of spice.

TIP
While this recipe takes only a few minutes, it's essential to keep the popcorn moving throughout. Make sure all the kernels are spread out on the bottom of the pan as they heat in the oil, and keep shaking the pan so they cook evenly. The same applies when you add the cheese and pepper – keep the popcorn moving so that it's evenly coated.

EVOO TO PAIR
Although inspired by our early-harvest Galega oil from Portugal, Tuscan varieties or Nocellaras from Sicily would also go well.

Place a large saucepan over a medium heat. Pour in 2 tablespoons of the oil and add 2 popcorn kernels to test the temperature. Cover the saucepan with a lid and wait patiently until the kernels pop. Watch closely so it doesn't smoke or burn.

Once the test kernels have popped, remove the pan from the heat and discard the popped kernels.

Pour the remaining popcorn kernels into the pan, replace the lid, and give the pan a gentle shake to ensure the kernels are evenly coated. Allow the pan to rest for about 1 minute so that the oil settles at the ideal temperature. This is important so it doesn't burn. Return the pan to a medium heat. As the kernels begin to pop, give the pan an occasional shake to help them cook evenly.

When the popping becomes active and loud, slightly tilt the lid to allow steam to escape – this little adjustment is key to achieving that perfect crunch.

Continue cooking until the popping slows to roughly one pop every few seconds. If the popcorn starts to overflow, simply transfer the upper portion to a bowl and return the pan to the heat. Once the popping has nearly stopped, remove the lid and carefully empty the popcorn into a large serving bowl.

Working quickly, sprinkle the popcorn with the cheese (or nutritional yeast) and season generously with pepper and a pinch of salt. (Speed is important to prevent all the melting cheese sinking to the bottom.) Drizzle with the remaining EVOO and mix well. Enjoy immediately.

Soups
& Salads

'Our olive oils are like our children,
they have life. We love them, we are proud
of them and we do our best to keep them safe from
things that might harm them, with a sense of
responsibility that a parent has.'

—Marianna Devetzoglou, producer, expert taster and olive oil guide, Oleosophia, Corinthia, Greece

Lentil & Rice Salad
with Herbs

Do as the Greeks do, and make a salads that don't have any lettuce in them at all. Focus instead on seasonal ingredients that pack a heavier punch, but still cover them in fresh herbs, with a tangy dressing. This combination of lentils, rice, herbs and a 'soupy' lemon and EVOO dressing is a great example. It's a staple meal that our farmer (and my husband's Greek godfather) in central Crete, Dimitris Fragkiadoulakis, often makes for lunch, or when in need of something quick and easy, but filling and nutritious.

Serves 4

- 100g (3½oz) white, brown or red rice
- 100g (3½oz) dried green, black or Puy lentils
- 4 ripe tomatoes, cored and diced
- 3 spring onions, thinly sliced
- 3 tablespoons roughly chopped dill
- 2 tablespoons roughly chopped flat leaf parsley
- 4–5 tablespoons extra virgin olive oil
- juice of 1 lemon
- splash of red or white wine vinegar
- salt and freshly ground black pepper

Cook the rice in salted boiling water according to the packet instructions, then drain and cool quickly under cold running water.

Meanwhile, cook the lentils according to the packet instructions, then drain and cool.

Transfer the cooled rice and lentils to a large bowl.

Add the tomatoes and spring onions to the rice mixture along with the herbs.

Add the EVOO, lemon juice and vinegar, and season well with salt and pepper. Mix to combine, making sure the dressing is pooling like a soup. This means it's been super-absorbed by the rice and lentil mixture and can be spooned up like soup or mopped up with bread.

MAKE IT YOUR OWN
Use whatever type of rice and lentils you have or prefer. Brown rice and black lentils will make a nuttier salad, while red rice is even more flavoursome.
When time is tight, you can use a drained 400g (14oz) can of lentils and swap the tomatoes for diced red peppers, roasted or raw, whichever you prefer.
Apple cider vinegar can be used in place of wine vinegar.
For extra vibrancy, add some thinly sliced preserved lemon and chopped fresh mint.
To make the salad a more substantial meal, you could add other pulses and legumes, such as chickpeas or beans, or add some cooked vegetables, such as courgettes or aubergines.

TIP
You can make this salad in advance for weekday lunches and keep it in the fridge for up to 3 days. Add a little extra dressing just before serving.

EVOO TO PAIR
Koroneiki, Lianolia, Arbequina or Cornicabra.

Apple & Squash Soup
with Spiced Kale & Nut Granola

Apple crumble or soup? Why not both? Created by Theresa von Wangenheim (aka @sssssoupssss on Instagram) for our Olive Oil Club, this recipe is an innovative pairing of spiced kale and nut granola. The latter can be made with any mixture of nuts – walnuts, pecans, almonds, hazelnuts and cashews are all good. The granola makes more than you need for this recipe, but keeps well for about 2 weeks if stored in an airtight container. Use it to top pasta, noodles, eggs or roasted vegetables.

Serves 4–6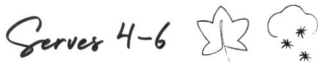

- 1 red kuri or butternut squash
- 2 crisp eating apples, such as Braeburn
- 4 tablespoons extra virgin olive oil, plus extra to serve
- 1 large onion, sliced
- 1 large garlic clove, crushed
- 1 teaspoon ground cumin
- 1 teaspoon crushed dried chilli flakes
- 1 litre (1¾ pints) chicken or vegetable stock
- 100ml (3½fl oz) crème fraîche
- salt and freshly ground black pepper

MAKE IT YOUR OWN
Find your ideal mix of nuts and seeds.

EVOO TO PAIR
Arbequina or Galega can play nicely into the apple notes.

Start by making the granola, which can be prepared ahead of time and stored in an airtight container until needed.

Preheat the oven to 180°C (160°C fan/350°F/Gas mark 4). Line a baking tray with nonstick baking paper.

Finely chop the kale and spread out in a single layer on the prepared tray. Drizzle with 2 tablespoons of the EVOO, season with the sea salt flakes and some freshly ground black pepper, and toss the kale to coat in the oil. Roast for about 10 minutes, until the kale is crisp and just beginning to brown.

Meanwhile, combine the nuts, seeds and spices in a bowl. Add the maple syrup and the remaining tablespoon EVOO, then mix to combine.

Transfer the kale to a bowl and set aside.

Spread the spiced nuts and seeds on the lined baking tray and roast for about 10 minutes, or until crisp and golden.

Add the crispy kale to the nut mixture and roast for 5 more minutes, until everything is crisp. Leave to cool completely, then store in an airtight container until needed.

To make the soup, preheat the oven to 200°C (180°C fan/ 400°F/Gas mark 6).

If using kuri squash, carefully slice off both ends, cut in half lengthways and scoop out the seeds. If using butternut squash, peel off the skin, then cut the flesh into chunky dice. Peel, core and roughly chop the apples.

FOR THE GRANOLA

- 125g (4½oz) kale, washed and dried
- 3 tablespoons extra virgin olive oil
- 125g (4½oz) mixed nuts, roughly chopped
- 50g (1¾oz) pumpkin seeds
- 35g (1¼oz) flax seeds
- 35g (1¼oz) sesame seeds
- ½–1 teaspoon coriander seeds, lightly crushed
- ½–1 teaspoon cumin seeds, lightly crushed
- ½ teaspoon crushed dried chilli flakes (optional)
- 2 tablespoons maple syrup
- 1 teaspoon sea salt flakes

Tip the squash and apples onto a lined baking tray, drizzle with 2 tablespoons of the EVOO, then season and roast for about 25 minutes, until slightly softened.

Meanwhile, place the remaining 2 tablespoons olive oil in a large saucepan over a medium heat. Add the onion and cook for 7–10 minutes, stirring often, until soft, translucent and fragrant. Add the garlic, cumin and chilli flakes and cook for a few more minutes.

Add the roasted squash and apples to the pan, pour in 800ml (23fl oz) of the stock and bring to the boil. Reduce the heat to a simmer and cook for another 15 minutes, until everything is softened.

Remove from the heat and blend until smooth, adding more stock if needed to loosen. Season to taste.

Serve the soup in bowls, adding a spoonful of crème fraîche to each one. Sprinkle with granola and add a drizzle of EVOO.

Green Gazpacho

Just what you need to cool down after a long day in the sun, and to get in a healthy quota of greens. Packed full of herbs, this soup has loads of fresh flavours going on and can be prepped in under 10 minutes. It feels both rich and refreshing. If you can find them, use baby cucumbers, as their flavour is often more intense than standard cucumbers. We served this soup created by our team member Frides O'Neill in shot glasses at our summer pop-up in Notting Hill, so it's also great for events or garden parties.

Serves 6

- 1 large avocado, peeled and roughly chopped
- 2 friggitelli peppers or 1 sweet green pepper, deseeded and roughly chopped
- 1 mild–medium hot green chilli, deseeded and roughly chopped
- 4 baby cucumbers, roughly chopped
- 1 garlic clove, crushed
- 130g (4½oz) young leaf spinach
- ½ small bunch of flat leaf parsley, leaves picked
- ½ small bunch of basil
- ½ small bunch of coriander
- 70g (2½oz) cashews, toasted
- 20ml (4 teaspoons) white wine vinegar
- 50ml (2fl oz) extra virgin olive oil, plus extra to serve
- 200–300ml (7–10fl oz) very cold water
- salt and freshly ground black pepper

Tip the prepared vegetables into a blender or food processor. Add the garlic, spinach, herbs and toasted cashews. Pour in the vinegar and EVOO, and season with salt and pepper.

Blend on high speed until everything is roughly chopped, then slowly add the water (you might not need it all) while blending continuously, until the gazpacho is smooth and reaches the desired consistency.

Taste and adjust the seasoning, then cover and chill for 1 hour, until cold.

Taste again after chilling and adjust as necessary. Serve in little glasses with a drizzle of EVOO.

MAKE IT YOUR OWN
Don't feel you must follow the recipe exactly. Throw in all the herbs you like – dill is a good addition – and almonds can be used in place of the cashews.

TIP
If kept cold, this soup holds its colour and flavour really well for up to 2 days.

EVOO TO PAIR
Styles like Cobrançosa, Mallorquina, Biancolillla or Arbequina.

Purslane Salad

Cana and Mey Cezairli are sisters who were born to Turkish parents in Germany. Together, they now have a beautiful olive grove in Milas, southeastern Turkey, and make their own oil from the local Memecik variety of olives. There's a lot of crossover between recipes from this part of the world, with classics such as stuffed peppers and rice rolls sharing the same base, but all the dishes contain elements from their respective cultures, which shine through. In this simple summer salad, known as semiz otu salatasi in Turkish, the components could be from almost anywhere, until you notice the pomegranate molasses, which indicates an origin in the Levant with its eastern Mediterranean notes.

 Serves 2

- 1 bunch of purslane, roughly chopped (see Tip)
- 1 peach, thinly sliced
- leaves from 2 sprigs basil
- 50g (1¾oz) walnuts, broken into pieces
- 4 tablespoons extra virgin olive oil
- 1 tablespoon pomegranate molasses
- salt

Place the purslane in a salad bowl, arrange the peach slices on top, then sprinkle with the basil leaves and walnut pieces.

Pour the EVOO into a small bowl, add the pomegranate molasses and a pinch of salt and mix well. Pour this dressing over the salad ingredients and toss to combine.

MAKE IT YOUR OWN
You often find variations of semiz otu salatasi with garlicky yogurt dressings – well worth a try.

TIP
If you can't find purslane, the best alternatives are lamb's lettuce and watercress.

EVOO TO PAIR
Use Memecik or other Turkish varieties, or opt for more delicate and grassy styles.

Pasta e Ceci

This recipe for chickpea and pasta soup is from one of the most respected mentors in the olive oil world, Johnny Madge: 'There are many versions of this Roman soup. Adding just one or two anchovies brings an amazing umami to what is a very simple recipe.'

Serves 4

- **200g (7oz) dried chickpeas, or 2 x 400g (14oz) jars or cans of chickpeas (see Tips below)**
- **3 garlic cloves, 1 whole and 2 finely chopped**
- **2 small sprigs of rosemary**
- **3 tablespoons extra virgin olive oil, plus extra to serve**
- **2 anchovies in oil**
- **1 tomato, skinned and chopped, or 1 teaspoon tomato purée**
- **150g (5½oz) ditalini or any other small soup pasta**
- **salt and freshly ground black pepper**
- **freshly grated Parmesan cheese, to serve**

MAKE IT YOUR OWN
For some earthy heat, add a pinch of chilli powder or smoked paprika with the anchovies.

TIPS
If using cans or jars of chickpeas, add 1 litre (1¾ pints) of hot water or light stock along with the garlic and rosemary and heat for a few minutes, then pick up the recipe from step 2. Don't have any small soup pasta? Simply break whatever type you have into small bits.

EVOO TO PAIR
Aromatic olive oils are spectacular on pasta e ceci, as the heat of the soup releases all the gorgeous aromas.

If using dried chickpeas, you will need to soak them for 12 hours or overnight in a large bowl of water. The next day, drain and rinse the chickpeas, tip them into a large pan and add 1.5 litres (2½ pints) water, the whole garlic clove and 1 sprig of rosemary; the water needs to cover the chickpeas by at least 4cm (1½in), so choose your pan size accordingly. Bring to the boil, using a spoon to remove any scum that floats to the surface. Reduce the heat and simmer for about 45 minutes, until the chickpeas are tender. Do not drain, as you will use the cooking water in the soup.

Pour the EVOO into a large saucepan and add the chopped garlic, the anchovies, remaining rosemary sprig and the tomato or tomato purée. Place the pan over a low heat to avoid burning the anchovies, as that will make the soup bitter. Stir until the anchovies have dissolved into the oil, ready to give their magical umami to the whole soup.

Using a slotted spoon, add the chickpeas to the soup pan and cook over a low heat for about 5 minutes so they soak up the deliciously flavoured oil.

Add about 1 litre (1¾ pints) of the chickpea cooking water and season with salt and pepper to taste. Bring to the boil, then simmer over a low heat for 10 minutes to bring the flavours together.

Now add the pasta to the soup and cook until just softer than al dente. The cooking time will vary depending on the type of pasta used. Add a little more of the chickpea water if the soup is looking slightly dry.

Ladle the soup into bowls and serve sprinkled with freshly grated Parmesan and a good drizzle of EVOO.

Cabbage & Lemon Slaw

Another humble dish that I first experienced in the middle of a Greek olive grove at harvest time. Maria Amargiotaki brought this out to us for lunch, and as we sat among the trees enjoying it with an omelette, I remember thinking how simple yet delicious this slaw was. What gives it the edge is the thin slices of lemon soaked into the mix, and the generous amount of olive oil that only a woman from a hillside village in Crete would dream of pouring for a single dish. It's another example of a nutrient-dense, fresh and fuss-free, cold-weather classic that our bodies truly need during the darker months. Also, it's quite cheap and cheerful.

Serves 6

- **1 small head of green cabbage, trimmed and outside leaves removed**
- **1 large unwaxed lemon**
- **5 tablespoons extra virgin olive oil, plus extra to serve**
- **salt and freshly ground black pepper**

Quarter and core the cabbage, cut into very thin shreds and place in a large bowl.

Cut the lemon in half and squeeze the juice over the cabbage.

Slice 1 of the squeezed lemon halves into thin slivers and add to the bowl.

Add the olive oil, season with salt and a generous grinding of pepper, and mix well to combine. Cover and set aside for 15–30 minutes to allow the acid from the lemons to slightly soften the cabbage.

Mix again before serving and swirl another drizzle of EVOO over the top.

MAKE IT YOUR OWN
Adding chopped fresh herbs, such as dill or mint, will freshen up this salad, while a little crushed garlic will deepen the flavour.
If the lemons aren't bright enough for your taste, apple cider or wine vinegar can be used as well.

TIPS
Green cabbage works better than red, but try whatever leaves you have on hand.
The slaw also pairs nicely with smoked salmon or oily fish, such as sardines or anchovies.

EVOO TO PAIR
Koroneiki, Lianolia or even an early-harvest Galega.

Orange Salad

The Italians do it with pepper. The Spanish add a little sugar. The Sicilians might add herbs. Martha Stewart even threw her hat into the ring with a version that adds chopped green olives. Any way you want it, it's time to pour fresh EVOO over some orange slices. Both are bursting with flavour in the late winter. Serve as a starter or a dessert, depending on your lifestyle. We like to think of the version below as a 'dessert salad'.

Serves 2

- 2 oranges
- 1 tablespoon caster sugar
- ½ teaspoon ground cinnamon
- 2–3 tablespoons extra virgin olive oil
- mint or basil, to garnish

Peeling and prepping the oranges is the only bit of this recipe that requires effort. To start, use a sharp knife to cut off the top and bottom of each fruit. Stand them on a flat end and slice downwards from top to bottom, following the natural curve of the orange, to remove both skin and pith. Repeat all the way around .

Slice the peeled oranges into circles and arrange on plates. Sprinkle each slice with sugar and cinnamon, then drizzle with EVOO. Garnish with fresh mint or basil and serve immediately.

MAKE IT YOUR OWN
For a more indulgent dessert, add a drizzle of melted dark chocolate and/or a dollop of cream.
Skip the sugar and cinnamon, and make a savoury salad with thinly sliced red onion, fresh basil, a squeeze of lemon juice and a pinch of chilli flakes. Seasoning the oranges with red onion, pomegranate seeds and freshly ground black pepper (as shown opposite) is also popular.

TIP
The point is to add interest to something at its peak of freshness, so serve with whatever you're in the mood for.

EVOO TO PAIR
For something light, opt for Arbequina, Biancolilla or Megaritiki. If you fancy a more fruity/spicy flavour, Hojiblanca is perfect.

Avgolemono Soup

Pronounced 'ahv-go-le-mo-no', this Greek soup is a godsend during the winter, and can be made in less than half an hour. The combination of simple chicken broth, lemon and egg makes a cream-like soup that's easy to bulk up with vegetables and herbs. The zesty flavour fills the gap left by tangy tomato soup at the end of summer. To ensure authenticity, I asked Maria – our dear family friend and producer in Crete – to weigh in with her tips, so this recipe is the real thing.

Serves 6–8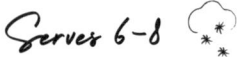

- 1–2 carrots, finely chopped
- 1–2 celery sticks, finely chopped
- ½ onion, finely chopped
- 3 tablespoons extra virgin olive oil, plus extra to drizzle
- 2–3 garlic cloves, crushed
- 2 litres (3½ pints) chicken stock
- 2 bay leaves
- 175g (6oz) short-grain rice
- 2 large eggs
- 125ml (4fl oz) freshly squeezed lemon juice
- handful of chopped parsley or basil
- salt and freshly ground black pepper

OPTIONAL EXTRAS
- shredded cooked chicken
- cooked diced potatoes
- shredded cabbage

Put the carrots, celery, onion and EVOO into a large saucepan. Place the pan over a medium heat and sauté for about 8 minutes, until the vegetables are tender but not coloured. Add the garlic and cook for a minute more.

Pour in the stock, add the bay leaves and bring to the boil. Now stir in the rice and season with salt and pepper. Reduce the heat to low and simmer for 15–20 minutes, until the rice is tender.

Now for the fun part. In a mixing bowl, whisk the eggs and lemon juice together until combined. Continue to whisk while slowly adding 2 ladlefuls of the stock – this will temper the lemon and egg mixture before the next step.

Place the stock pan over a low heat, stir in the egg mixture, then immediately remove from the heat. The soup will thicken, becoming creamy and silky.

Spoon into bowls, garnish with chopped parsley or basil, and drizzle with extra EVOO. At this point you can also add any extra herbs, cooked chicken or vegetables.

TIPS
Maria offers the following advice: 'Pass the finished soup through a strainer to remove any small bits. For extra tang, I like to add slivers of lemon rind, as we do in our cabbage and green winter salads.'

EVOO TO PAIR
Nocellara, Koroneiki, Cornicabra and Istrian varieties are lovely here.

MAKE IT YOUR OWN
Add any fresh herbs or spices you have to hand. A little chopped chilli or a few chilli flakes could spice things up.
Top everything with toasted sesame seeds or fried garlic flakes.

Black-Eyed Bean Soup
Soupa Louvana

Nicolas Nétien is one of the most respected producers of extremely high-polyphenol EVOOs in the world. Though French, he has been based in Cyprus for years, where he works with small-scale growers. When asked about the go-to recipe to represent his region, he said: 'This is very Cypriot. Most foods here are either Turkish, Greek or Middle Eastern, but the louvi [black-eyed bean] is a staple on the island.' In Cyprus, you're likely to find this soup served with olives and toasted bread.

Serves 2

- **275g (9¾oz) dried black-eyed beans**
- **3 tablespoons extra virgin olive oil, plus extra to serve**
- **1 onion, finely chopped or coarsely grated**
- **2–3 garlic cloves, crushed**
- **2–3 bay leaves**
- **1 teaspoon dried oregano**
- **100g (3½oz) long-grain rice**
- **juice of 1 lemon**
- **salt and freshly ground black pepper**

MAKE IT YOUR OWN
Chopped greens, such as chard, spinach or courgettes, could be added for the last 5 minutes of cooking time, and perhaps some chopped herbs, such as parsley or dill.

EVOO TO PAIR
Choose something from the region, such as Kypriaki, Ladolea or Dopia – though a Koroneiki, which is easier to find, would work great too. Whichever you use, make sure it's an early-harvest oil to get some punchy notes.

Soak the black-eyed beans in a large bowl of cold water for 8 hours or overnight.

The next day rinse the beans under cold running water and place in a saucepan. Pour over enough water to cover the beans by about 3cm (1¼in), place over a medium heat and bring to the boil. Lower the heat and simmer for 5–10 minutes, skimming off any scum as it rises to the surface. Drain the beans and rinse the pan.

Heat the EVOO in the saucepan over low–medium heat, add the onion and crushed garlic and sauté for about 5 minutes, until softened and the onion takes on a little colour.

Add the bay leaves and oregano, and return the beans to the pan. Pour in enough water to cover the beans by 3–4cm (1¼–1½in). Bring to the boil, reduce the heat to a simmer and cook for about 40 minutes, or until the beans are tender.

Add the rice to the pan and top up with enough water to cover by about 3cm (1¼in). Season well with salt and pepper, and continue simmering on a low heat for another 12–15 minutes, or until the rice is just cooked.

Add lemon juice to taste and check the seasoning.

Serve in bowls with a good drizzle of EVOO.

Marianna's Fasolada

'Fasolada is a traditional Greek soup of white beans, olive oil and vegetables, such as carrots, celery, onion and perhaps tomato,' says Marianna Devetzoglou of Oleosophia groves near Corinthia. 'It belongs to a group of foods we call ladera, meaning that they are consumed with olive oil. During autumn and winter, my yiayia [grandma] would make fasolada every Wednesday or Friday for religious reasons, as those days are meant to be meat-free. It is healthy, colourful and comforting – typical yiayia food.' It goes well with feta cheese and fresh bread.

Serves 6–8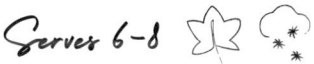

- **250g (9oz) dried white beans, such as cannellini**
- **4 tablespoons extra virgin olive oil, plus more to drizzle**
- **1 large onion, chopped**
- **2 celery sticks, chopped**
- **2 carrots, diced**
- **2 garlic cloves, crushed**
- **400g (14oz) chopped fresh tomatoes, or 400g (14oz) can chopped tomatoes**
- **1 bay leaf**
- **500ml (18fl oz) light vegetable stock or water**
- **salt and freshly ground black pepper**

TO SERVE
- **feta cheese**
- **bread**

MAKE IT YOUR OWN
Lean into the veggies with more greens or even corn, or throw in a protein of your choice (sausage goes nicely here).

EVOO TO PAIR
Koroneiki, Olympia, Tsounati.

Rinse the beans, place in a large bowl and cover with plenty of cold water. Leave to soak overnight at room temperature.

The next morning drain the beans, tip them into a large saucepan and pour in enough cold water to cover them by 3–4cm (1¼in–1½in). Bring to the boil over a medium heat and use a slotted spoon to remove any scum that rises to the surface. Reduce the heat to a simmer and cook the beans for 45–60 minutes, or until tender.

In the meantime, heat the oil in a flameproof casserole dish over a low–medium heat. Add the onion, celery and carrots and sauté for 8–10 minutes, until softened. Stir in the garlic and cook for another minute.

Add the tomatoes and bay leaf, season well with salt and pepper and continue to cook until the tomatoes break down into a sauce.

Drain the beans and add to the tomato mixture. Pour in enough vegetable stock or water to cover the beans by about 2cm (¾in) and cover the pan with a lid. Reduce the heat and simmer for about 30 minutes, until the beans are soft. During this time the beans should be just covered with the sauce at all times, so add more stock or hot water, a little at a time, as required.

When cooked, take off the heat and drizzle over more EVOO. Serve hot in winter and at room temperature in summer, ideally with bread and feta cheese.

Apple Salmorejo

While climate change has intensified things, blisteringly hot summers have always been part of life in the south of Spain. The cold soups of Andalucía are a delight on hot days. Salmorejo, with bread in the mix, is a more filling and meal-like option than the lighter gazpacho. This recipe comes to us from Alexis Kerner, an American who's been living in Spain for more than 25 years. Based in Seville, Alexis is an international olive oil judge, environmentalist and educator who founded The Olive Oil Workshop, which organizes tastings and tours of the regional olive oil and cuisine.

Serves 4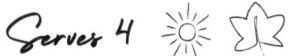

- 2 thick slices of dense country bread or sourdough
- 2 green apples, peeled, cored and roughly chopped
- 2 golden apples, peeled, cored and roughly chopped
- ½ small head of fennel, trimmed and roughly chopped, fronds reserved
- 1 garlic clove
- 2 generous handfuls rocket (about 50g/1¾oz in total)
- 100ml (3½fl oz) fruity, peppery extra virgin olive oil, plus extra to serve
- generous pinch of sea salt flakes
- 3–4 ice cubes
- 3–4 tablespoons cold water, as needed

  TO SERVE (OPTIONAL)
- 75g (2¾oz) goats' cheese, crumbled
- 40g (1½oz) pine nuts, toasted

Remove the crusts from the bread and cut the remainder into cubes; you will need around 50g (1¾oz).

Toss the bread, apples, fennel, garlic and rocket into a blender or food processor, add the EVOO and salt and blend until nearly smooth.

Add the ice cubes and trickle in 2–3 tablespoons cold water. Blend again until smooth. The goal is a silky, spoonable texture, so add water a bit at a time to achieve this.

Taste and adjust the seasoning. More salt? More olive oil? You're the judge.

Serve the soup cold, adding a swirl of olive oil and some reserved fennel fronds to each and topping with crumbled goats' cheese and/or toasted pine nuts if you wish.

MAKE IT YOUR OWN
Use this recipe as a base and build on it: a sprig of mint, a sliver of avocado, or even a shaving of Manchego cheese would all be lovely additions.
Don't overthink it – this is a 'use what you have' kind of recipe. Just let the apples shine and the olive oil carry it home.

TIP
If you're making this ahead, a splash of lemon juice helps prevent the apples from discolouring.

EVOO TO PAIR
Choose a fruity oil with balance and bite – Arbequina for softness, or a Hojiblanca if you want to play up the peppery finish.

Claudia's Tabbouli

I ate tabbouli (or tabbouleh) a lot as a kid, thanks to the influence of a Lebanese community where I grew up in Texas. Coming from the heart of the Levant, this salad has the flavours of that region, but similar salads come from many Mediterranean and Middle Eastern countries. This version comes to us from Claudia Hanna, a micro-producer with olive trees in Cyprus. She also hosts the podcast 'If This Food Could Talk: History for Everyone Who Eats' and takes people on travel excursions across the Eastern Mediterranean to discover the various cultures and their intersections through dishes like this one.

Serves 4

- 100g (3½oz) regular or wholewheat couscous, or quinoa or fine bulgur wheat
- 3 spring onions, trimmed and finely chopped
- 2 tomatoes, finely chopped
- 1 small English or Persian cucumber, finely chopped
- 2–3 bunches (about 100g/3½oz) flat leaf parsley, finely chopped
- 4 tablespoons extra virgin olive oil
- juice of ½ lemon
- salt and freshly ground black pepper

TO SERVE (OPTIONAL)
- feta cheese
- pickled green chillies

Pour 250ml (9fl oz) water into a saucepan, bring to the boil, then remove from the heat. Add the couscous, stir to combine and cover the pan with a lid. Set aside for about 10 minutes to soften and absorb all the water.

Meanwhile, place the spring onions, tomatoes, cucumber and parsley in a large bowl. Add the couscous, EVOO and lemon juice, and season well with salt and pepper. Stir to combine, then chill and enjoy!

Serve with feta cheese and pickled green chillies, if you like.

MAKE IT YOUR OWN
I like my tabbouleh a little spicy, so I add red chilli pepper paste to give it an extra kick.
Try adding sliced pickled chillies or some pomegranate seeds for a pop of colour.
You could also add chopped mint or rocket as well as the parsley.

EVOO TO PAIR
Varieties like Kypriaki, Ladoelia from Cyprus, Kalamon from Greece or Spanish Hojiblanca.

Watermelon Salad

There's really no wrong way to make this salad, which is something we love in a recipe. It can be as simple as combining watermelon, EVOO and basil, or you can lean into a theme. Here we've gone Greek (surprise!) to balance out the sweetness of the melon with the bitterness of the Kalamata olives and oil. I make many variations of watermelon salad throughout the fruit's short summer window, but I keep coming back to this one.

Serves 4

- 1 small watermelon
- 1 cucumber
- 2 large ripe tomatoes
- 1 small red onion, thinly sliced
- 200g (7oz) feta cheese, roughly diced
- 100–150g (3½–5½oz) pitted Kalamata olives
- handful of basil, leaves picked
- handful of mint, leaves picked
- 3 tablespoons red wine or balsamic vinegar
- 6 tablespoons extra virgin olive oil
- salt and freshly ground black pepper

Peel the watermelon and cut into large chunks. Cut the cucumber and tomatoes into similar-sized pieces. Place them all in a large, pretty bowl, then add the red onion and feta.

Squeeze the olives with your fingers or squish them on a chopping board with your palm to open them up. Add to the bowl.

Now tear the herb leaves, or keep them whole if you prefer, and add to the salad.

Mix the vinegar and olive oil in a small bowl and season with salt and pepper.

Pour the dressing over the salad, mix gently to combine and serve.

MAKE IT YOUR OWN
Try adding avocado and lime instead of the vinegar.
For a stronger salad vibe, add rocket or watercress.
Make it spicy by adding chillies or Tajín (Mexican) seasoning, or give it a lighter kick with fried shallots.

TIP
This salad needs to be eaten very soon after it's made, so if making it in advance for a group of people, prep all the ingredients, but keep the dressing and cheese in their own containers until you're ready to mix and serve.

EVOO TO PAIR
Koroneiki, Galega or Leccino.

Caesar Radicchio Salad

Another recipe from my mother's arsenal, this salad has a dressing that is not for the faint of heart. The woman is keeping vampires away with most of her cooking, so I'm warning you now that there's a lot of tang from garlic, the lemon and anchovies. I've paired this dressing with more interesting winter salad leaves for serving when citrus fruit shines and we need more exciting dressings for our food.

Serves 4

- 4 slices of sourdough bread
- 150ml (5fl oz) extra virgin olive oil
- 2 heads of radicchio
- 4 anchovy fillets in oil
- 3 garlic cloves, crushed
- 1 large egg yolk
- 1 tablespoon Dijon mustard
- 2 teaspoons Worcestershire sauce
- 1–2 tablespoons lemon juice
- 50g (1¾oz) Parmesan cheese, grated, plus extra to serve
- salt and freshly ground black pepper

MAKE IT YOUR OWN
Swap out or add kale to the mix, or try adding shaved Brussels sprouts. Dried cranberries also balance out the tartness of the dressing.

TIPS
This salad does not keep well, so serve it immediately.
If the egg yolk isn't your thing, use 1 tablespoon mayonnaise instead.

EVOO TO PAIR
You could lean into the pepperiness and bitterness of this salad by using a Tuscan oil, such as Frantoio, or keep it milder with a Greek Manaki.

Preheat the oven to 190°C (170°C fan/375°F/Gas mark 5).

Cut or tear the bread into 2cm (¾in) pieces and place in a roasting tray. Drizzle with 2 tablespoons of the EVOO, season with salt and mix with your hands to coat the bread in the oil. Place in the oven for about 10 minutes, until the croutons are crisp and golden brown. Set aside until needed.

Remove any wilted outer leaves from the radicchio and quarter them lengthways. Separate the remaining leaves, wash in cold water and pat dry. Keep in the fridge until needed.

Now make the dressing. Using a mortar and pestle, or a bowl and fork, mash the anchovy fillets and garlic into a paste. Add the egg yolk, mustard, Worcestershire sauce and lemon juice and mix well with the pestle or fork.

Whisk in the remaining 120ml (3¾fl oz) EVOO and the Parmesan. Season to taste with salt and pepper. Taste and add more lemon juice, Worcestershire sauce or mustard, as you like.

Tip the radicchio leaves into a large salad bowl, add the dressing and mix to coat the leaves evenly. Sprinkle with extra Parmesan and the croutons, and serve immediately.

Hearty Chickpea Broth
with Whipped Tahini

We're massive fans of plant-based chef Kali Jago. She shared this recipe with us on a cold winter's day and it instantly became a favourite. 'On a trip to Athens, I ate at Diporto, a no-frills, no-menu restaurant where you're served a selection of dishes without ordering,' Kali explains. 'Among them was this dish: a simple broth, melt-in-the-mouth jumbo chickpeas, lots of black pepper and plenty of extra virgin olive oil. It was heavenly! I had to re-create it – and I'm happy to say this version is pretty much spot on.' Oil from Corinthia is perfect for this dish: while it's delicate, it adds depth and richness, bringing everything together beautifully. Don't be shy with it, as a good EVOO really makes the humble pulse sing. For an extra dose of goodness, this works beautifully with kale, savoy cabbage or other leafy greens. The soup is topped with a dollop of whipped tahini, a delicious addition that's also great with other dishes.

Serves 6

- **2 small onions, sliced**
- **125ml (4fl oz) Greek extra virgin olive oil, plus more for drizzling**
- **4 large garlic cloves, crushed**
- **2 x 540g (1lb 3oz) jars Bold Bean Co queen chickpeas, or 2 x 400g (14oz) cans good-quality chickpeas plus 500ml (18fl oz) light vegetable stock**
- **3 fresh bay leaves**
- **juice of 1 lemon**
- **50g (1¾oz) flat leaf parsley, leaves picked**
- **salt and freshly ground black pepper**
- **fresh bread, to serve**

  FOR THE WHIPPED TAHINI
- **50g (1¾oz) tahini**
- **2 tablespoons extra virgin olive oil**
- **juice of ½ lemon**

Place the onions in a large saucepan, then add 3 tablespoons of the EVOO and a pinch of salt. Cook over a low–medium heat for about 10 minutes, until the onions are soft and starting to caramelize at the edges. Add the garlic and cook for another minute.

If using Bold Bean Co's queen chickpeas, add them and their liquid, along with 300ml (½ pint) water and the bay leaves. If using canned chickpeas, drain them and add to the pan with the vegetable stock and the bay leaves. Bring to the boil, add the remaining 100ml (3½fl oz) EVOO and cover with a lid. Reduce the heat and cook at a gentle simmer for about 40 minutes, until the onions are soft and mellow and the chickpeas are tender.

While the chickpeas are cooking, place the tahini, EVOO and lemon juice in a bowl and whisk to combine, or blitz them in a blender or food processor. Slowly add 50–100ml (2–3½fl oz) cold water, whisking continuously until the mixture is smooth and creamy. (The amount of water depends on the particular tahini you are using.) Add salt to taste and more lemon juice if needed.

MAKE IT YOUR OWN
This works beautifully with kale, savoy cabbage or other leafy greens.

EVOO TO PAIR
Oils from the Peloponnese, but also Istria, work well here.

Once the chickpeas are cooked, remove and discard the bay leaves, then add lemon juice to taste and season well with salt and pepper.

Sprinkle the picked parsley leaves over the chickpeas and serve in bowls, topped with the whipped tahini, a drizzle of EVOO and plenty of fresh bread to mop it all up.

Sun-Kissed Tuscan Tomato Soup

'I believe this is the best-ever recipe for tomato soup, and I have never met anyone who does not like it – children love it, too,' says Candice, who with her husband Fabrizio produces an excellent Tuscan olive oil at the Olea Prilis groves in the Maremma region. 'Using sun-ripened tomatoes is important, but in the winter you can use those that have been preserved during the summer. The soup is packed with antioxidants from the tomatoes and olive oil, so it's really healthy. Of course, it should be served with bruschetta drizzled with olive oil.'

Serves 4

- 250ml (9fl oz) hot water
- 80ml (2¾fl oz) extra virgin olive oil, plus extra to serve
- 1 teaspoon vegetable stock powder
- 1kg (2lb 4oz) mini plum tomatoes
- handful of basil leaves, chopped
- 1 tablespoon balsamic vinegar
- salt and freshly ground black pepper

Put the water, EVOO and stock into a large saucepan and bring to the boil.

Add the tomatoes, reduce the heat and simmer until soft, 35–40 minutes, depending on the tomatoes used. Set aside to cool, then blend until smooth.

Add the chopped basil and balsamic vinegar to taste. Check the seasoning and add salt and pepper if needed.

In cold weather, serve straight away in small bowls with a drizzle of EVOO. Alternatively, leave to cool, then refrigerate and serve chilled on a warm summer's day.

MAKE IT YOUR OWN
To make the soup a bit more indulgent, blend 200ml (7fl oz) double cream into it after all the other ingredients have been blended.

TIPS
Use the best tomatoes you can find – ideally, datterini. Add cracked black pepper and a bit of lemon juice to ramp up the flavours, particularly if the tomatoes aren't at their best.

EVOO TO PAIR
Choose Tuscan varieties, such as the classic blend of Frantoio, Leccino and Moraiolo.

Creamy Orange Gazpacho
Porra de Naranja

It was a chilly harvest night in Antequera, Spain, an hour outside Malaga, when I sat around a table with leading olive oil experts, an award-winning producer, a Michelin-starred chef from Denmark and this humble soup. Porra is a type of cold soup from the gazpacho family, and, like its cousins salmorejo and ajo blanco, is a classic bread, olive oil, vinegar and garlic combination – originally created to use up stale bread. The difference between gazpachos is often determined by region, but also by what is available in a particular season. Here we're sharing what might be considered the winter version, when historically tomatoes weren't available. I encountered it at the Arte de Cozina restaurant in Andalucía that November evening, when the first oranges were in season, and I fell in love with its vibrant flavour.

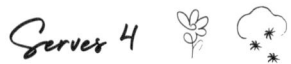

Serves 4

- 1 loaf of day-old sourdough bread
- 500ml (18fl oz) freshly squeezed orange juice, strained
- 1 garlic clove, crushed
- 50ml (2fl oz) extra virgin olive oil, plus extra to serve
- salt

Scoop out the doughy inside of the bread – you will need 500g (1lb 2oz) of it. Discard the crusts or save them for another use (see Tips below).

Tear the bread into pieces and place in a shallow bowl. Add the orange juice and leave to soak for a minute or two. Transfer to a blender, add the garlic, olive oil and a pinch of salt, and blitz until the mixture is smooth.

Pour into small bowls or cups and serve immediately with a swirl of EVOO across the top, or store in the fridge until needed.

MAKE IT YOUR OWN
Garnish with a sprinkle of cinnamon in the cooler months, or some mint leaves in the warmer ones.

TIPS
The fluffy centre of a baguette works well in this soup, but any bread with a dense crumb will do the trick.
You can toast the leftover crusts and blitz them into breadcrumbs to scatter on top of the soup for extra texture.

EVOO TO PAIR
Arbequina, Hojiblanca, Manaiki, Verdial or Lechín de Sevilla.

Big Batch Dressing

'A good salad dressing works wonders,' says plant-based chef Bettina Campolucci Bordi. 'And a tangy, tasty dressing that is available in your fridge at any given time is even better. This is a fantastic base that can be elevated with different add-ins when one version becomes boring.' It's important to have a go-to dressing in your arsenal – one that can be used for salads, as a dip for raw vegetables and even as a sauce over things like chicken and roasted veg. From a nutritional perspective, what a nice vinegar and EVOO can do when combined with plants is nothing short of magical. Do your gut and general health a favour: dress up your food.

Makes 350ml (12fl oz)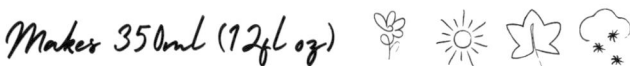

- 250ml (9fl oz) extra virgin olive oil
- 80ml (2¾fl oz) apple cider vinegar
- 1 tablespoon Dijon mustard
- 1 tablespoon maple syrup or runny honey
- salt and freshly ground black pepper

Place all the ingredients in a screwtop glass jar of a suitable size and shake well to combine.

This dressing will keep for up to a week in the fridge – a perfect chilled staple.

MAKE IT YOUR OWN
Try adding fresh herbs, such as finely chopped dill, chives, tarragon, basil or parsley. Or add a finely diced shallot or ¼ red onion.
Toasted sesame seeds or chilli flakes are good additions, as are capers and finely chopped gherkins.
Try swapping out the apple cider vinegar for any good wine or sherry vinegar. Adding smooth or grainy mustard works well too.

TIP
I love using recycled jars for this kind of thing.
A standard jam jar is the ideal size.

Vita-Slaw

This is the remedy for winter: a seasonal, vitamin-packed slaw that is bold, flavourful and healthy. The trinity of citrus, cabbage and carrots delivers a nutritious punch (hello, vitamin C!) that is really needed during the colder months. New-harvest olive oil weaves all the flavours together, bringing out the very best in these ingredients at their peak. I started making this as a healthy lunch while we were still running the business out of our home that first winter, inspired by the other cabbage salad (see page 74) Maria made for us that first harvest – and I come back to it every year.

Serves 4–6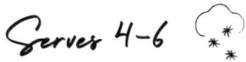

- ½ small head of white, green or red cabbage, finely shredded
- 2 carrots, coarsely grated
- 1 apple, coarsely grated
- 2 spring onions, trimmed and finely chopped
- small bunch of mint, leaves finely chopped

FOR THE DRESSING

- 5cm (2in) piece of fresh root ginger, peeled and finely grated
- finely grated zest of 1 unwaxed lemon or citrus fruit of your choice
- 4 tablespoons extra virgin olive oil
- 2 tablespoons apple cider vinegar
- 1 tablespoon good-quality runny honey
- ½ teaspoon ground turmeric
- salt and freshly ground black pepper

Tip all prepared slaw ingredients into a large bowl and mix well.

Place the ginger and lemon zest in a small bowl, add the remaining dressing ingredients and season well with salt and pepper. Whisk to combine, then pour the dressing over the slaw and mix thoroughly.

The slaw can be served immediately after preparing it, or covered and chilled for a couple of hours to allow all the flavours to combine.

MAKE IT YOUR OWN
To make a heartier salad, slice some grilled chicken and serve alongside the slaw or mixed into it. Grilled fish or even halloumi would also be great served with this slaw.

TIP
Slaws improve with keeping, so this is even better the next day.

EVOO TO PAIR
Choose an early-harvest oil that has a bitter or green flavour, over one that's later and sweeter.

Easy
Weekdays

'Good olive oil makes good food taste better.'

—Marije Passos, international olive oil judge and producer, Passeite Olive Oil, Coimbra, Portugal

Moqueca

This is a dish that speaks to Brazil's colourful culture, combining Portuguese, African and Indigenous influences. Marcelo Scofano, a Brazilian olive oil sensory analyst, shared this classic fish stew with us – a vibrant example of his homeland's cuisine.

Serves 6

- 900g–1kg (2lb–2lb 4oz) thick hake fillets, or similar firm white fish (cod, haddock, halibut or even monkfish are all good here), skinned and boned
- 2 limes
- 3 tablespoons extra virgin olive oil, plus extra to serve
- 1 onion, chopped
- 1 fat garlic clove, crushed
- 1 red chilli, deseeded and finely chopped
- 1½ teaspoons ground turmeric
- 1 red pepper, deseeded and diced
- 3 ripe tomatoes, roughly chopped
- 400ml (14fl oz) can coconut milk
- 100ml (3½fl oz) dry white wine
- 400ml (14fl oz) seafood or vegetable stock
- 300g (10½oz) prawns, peeled and deveined
- 3 tablespoons chopped fresh coriander and/or parsley
- salt and freshly ground black pepper

FOR THE RICE
- 2 tablespoons extra virgin olive oil
- 1 onion, finely chopped
- 1 garlic clove, crushed
- 300g (10½oz) long-grain white rice

Cut the fish into 4cm (1½in) pieces and place on a tray. Add the finely grated zest and juice from 1 lime, season with salt and mix to coat the fish. Cover and set aside.

Pour 2–3 tablespoons EVOO into a large sauté pan, add the onion and cook over a medium heat for about 5 minutes, stirring often until softened. Add the garlic, chilli and turmeric and cook for a further minute.

Add the red pepper and tomatoes and cook for a minute more, until just softened. Pour in the coconut milk and cook over a low heat for about 3 minutes, until slightly thickened, before adding the wine and stock. Bring to the boil, reduce to a simmer, then add the fish to the pan. Season with salt and pepper and cook for about 10 minutes over a low heat, until the fish is just cooked through. Add the prawns, cook for another minute, then remove the pan from the heat.

While the moqueca is cooking, prepare the rice. Heat the EVOO in a large saucepan, add the onion and garlic, and cook over a medium heat for about 5 minutes, until soft and just starting to caramelize. Add the rice and stir to coat in the oil. Pour in enough water to cover the rice by 3–4cm (1¼–1½in), add a pinch of salt and bring to the boil. Reduce to a simmer, half-cover the pan with a lid and cook for about 12 minutes, until the rice is tender.

Add half the chopped herbs to the fish and half to the rice. Cut the remaining lime into wedges.

Serve the moqueca and rice in shallow bowls, drizzle with EVOO and add lime wedges for squeezing over.

EVOO TO PAIR
Medium green to intense in flavour. Koroneiki, which grows well in Brazil, would be great here.

Chicken Piccata

This was a staple dish in my home when I was growing up in Texas, and is still one my mom makes regularly. It's very much an Italian-American recipe, generally made with chicken rather than the veal that would be used in Italy. That substitution aside, the flavours are like the bright, vibrant and zesty notes you find in places that also grow olives.

Serves 4

- 1 unwaxed lemon
- 2 large skinless, boneless chicken breasts
- 2–3 tablespoons plain flour
- 4 tablespoons extra virgin olive oil, plus extra to serve
- 2 garlic cloves, thinly sliced or finely chopped
- 2 tablespoons capers in brine, rinsed
- 100ml (3½fl oz) dry white wine
- 125ml (4fl oz) chicken stock
- 2–3 tablespoons roughly chopped flat leaf parsley
- salt and freshly ground black pepper

TO SERVE
- angel-hair pasta, orzo, rice or roast potatoes

Squeeze the juice from one half of the lemon and cut the other half into thin slices.

Slice the chicken breasts in half horizontally to make 4 thin cutlets. Season with salt and pepper on both sides. Lightly coat the chicken pieces in the flour and shake off the excess.

Place the EVOO in a frying pan over medium–high heat. Once hot, cook the chicken in batches for about 3 minutes per side, until golden and cooked through. Set aside on a plate.

Add the garlic and capers to the pan and cook for about 1 minute, until soft and just starting to turn golden. Add the lemon juice, lemon slices, wine and stock to the pan. Bring to a gentle boil, scraping up any browned bits from the bottom of the pan. Let the sauce reduce slightly for about 2 minutes.

Turn the heat to low and return the chicken to the pan, spooning the sauce over to coat it. Let it warm through for a minute or two, then stir in the parsley and drizzle with extra EVOO to serve.

Serve with your carb of choice, such as angel-hair pasta, orzo, rice or roast potatoes.

MAKE IT YOUR OWN
Swap the chicken for fish, such as cod, for a more Mediterranean vibe.
Try adding chopped olives and red peppers; it's also gorgeous with green beans.
My mom also adds garlic, but that's because she adds garlic to everything.

TIP
This can be made in a slow-cooker. Essentially, throw in everything except the parsley and base carbohydrate, and cook on low for 4–5 hours.

EVOO TO PAIR
Something citrusy and peppery, such as an early-harvest Picual, Nocellara or Picholine.

Beans, Greens & Feta

Ever since I came across this dish in a Paris wine bar called Buvette a few years ago, I haven't been able to shake it. It's a near-perfect parcel of all the nutrition you need, while also being surprisingly elegant. The most basic version is a combination of butter beans, lemon zest, a tiny bit of salt and a healthy pour of a strong EVOO. But like many simple dishes, you can make it your own. For me, that usually means adding greens and feta. Ready in a matter of minutes, this dish is a weekly lunch in my house, and will provide numerous health benefits when made a pillar of your diet.

Serves 2–3 as a main, or 4 as a side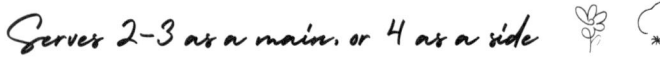

- 2 tablespoons extra virgin olive oil, plus extra for drizzling
- 200g (7oz) Tenderstem or purple sprouting broccoli, trimmed
- 200g (7oz) leafy spinach
- 570g (1lb 3oz) jar of butter beans, drained and rinsed (we love Bold Bean Co's Queen Butter Beans)
- 150g (5½oz) feta cheese
- finely grated zest of ½ unwaxed lemon
- sea salt flakes and freshly ground black pepper
- bread, to serve

Heat the EVOO in a sauté pan over a medium–high heat. Add the broccoli pieces and stir-fry for 3–4 minutes, until tender. Add the spinach and continue to cook for 1 minute, until the leaves have wilted.

Add the beans to the pan and cook for another 2 minutes, until they are heated through.

Spoon the beans and greens onto plates, crumble the feta over the top and drizzle generously with EVOO so that it pools around the beans.

Sprinkle with lemon zest and season with sea salt flakes and freshly ground black pepper. Serve with plenty of good bread to mop up the oil.

MAKE IT YOUR OWN
Throw in some sautéed garlic or onions.
Freshen it up with lemon juice or a bit of pesto.
Sprinkle with diced ham or chicken pieces to increase the protein content.

EVOO TO PAIR
I like this with something from Umbria, Tuscany or Andalucía.
A grassy, early Koroneiki always works, too.

Shaved Asparagus
with Pangrattato

This vibrant salad from plant-based chef Bettina Campolucci Bordi celebrates seasonal produce at its finest. It's one of those quietly brilliant recipes – no oven, no fuss, just a handful of good ingredients treated with a little care. 'The secret here is in the olive oil,' says Bettina. 'A quality EVOO brings the whole thing together, coating those fine asparagus ribbons and carrying the lemon perfectly. The golden, garlicky crunch of the pangrattato takes this dish from lovely to let's make this again tonight.'

Serves 2

- 1 large bunch of asparagus, woody stalks discarded
- finely grated zest and juice of 1 unwaxed lemon
- 4 tablespoons extra virgin olive oil
- 1 large slice or 2 small slices of day-old bread
- 1 garlic clove, crushed
- pinch of crushed dried chilli flakes
- leaves from 3 sprigs of thyme
- salt and freshly ground black pepper

Shave the asparagus spears into long thin strips using a vegetable peeler. Finely chop any remaining bits that are too thin to shave.

Place the asparagus in a bowl and add the lemon juice, half the zest and 2 tablespoons EVOO. Gently mix with your hands, massaging the oil and lemon into the asparagus to coat thoroughly. Set aside to marinate while you make the pangrattato.

Tear the bread into pieces and blitz in a blender or food processor to create breadcrumbs. Place a frying pan over a medium–high heat and add the remaining 2 tablespoons EVOO. Once the oil is hot, add the breadcrumbs, garlic, chilli flakes and thyme, and season with salt and pepper. Cook for a few minutes, stirring continuously until the breadcrumbs are crisp and golden. Turn off the heat, then stir in the remaining lemon zest.

Arrange the marinated asparagus in a lovely serving dish or on plates, top with the pangrattato and enjoy!

MAKE IT YOUR OWN
Add peas to build it out more, but I've also used this as a topping for pasta!

TIPS
You can prepare the asparagus in advance and let it marinate for longer than specified if you wish for a more intense flavour.
Here, we serve the pangrattato on top of the asparagus, but it's also nice to serve it underneath and mix it in at the last minute so that the asparagus stays super green and vibrant.

EVOO TO PAIR
This can do well with an earlier harvest oil with green notes.

Spaghetti
with Fresh Anchovies

'The best pasta is the simple one – just drizzled with bitter EVOO, lemon zest and Parmesan. But unfortunately, nobody is allowed to talk about the simplest recipe in Italy or in a recipe book.' This was the response when I asked Francesca Oliva for a pasta recipe to showcase the oil her family has been making for generations. Originally, I had in my head spaghetti alla Siracusana, the pasta of her region. But Francesca wanted to show that the oil can also be a sauce, so we trimmed down the ingredients to reflect the simplicity of what pasta can be in her part of Sicily.

Serves 4

- **450g (1lb) fresh anchovies**
- **350–400g (12–14oz) spaghetti**
- **3 tablespoons extra virgin olive oil, plus extra to serve**
- **1 large garlic clove, crushed**
- **75g (2¾oz) sun-dried tomatoes, roughly chopped**
- **2 tablespoons capers**
- **½ teaspoon dried oregano, plus extra to serve**
- **salt and freshly ground black pepper**

MAKE IT YOUR OWN
You can make a version of this recipe with canned anchovies, but do try to keep them whole and to the side until the end.
Add 2 tablespoons chopped parsley to the sauce.

TIP
Francesca says: 'I love spaghetti al dente and never cook it for more than 8 minutes.'

EVOO TO PAIR
Cerasuola, Nocellara del Belice, Tonda Iblea or Coratina.

Rub each anchovy under cold running water to remove the scales. Pinch off the heads, pull out the innards, then run your finger from the gills to the tail to open out the belly. Wash the inside again to remove any remaining entrails. Using your fingers, pinch the spine out from the head to the tail and remove the dorsal fin. Divide each fish into 2 fillets and pat dry on kitchen paper.

Bring a large pan of generously salted water to the boil. Add the spaghetti and cook until it is just shy of being al dente.

Meanwhile, about 3 minutes after you add the pasta to the boiling water, place the EVOO in a sauté pan over a medium heat, then add the garlic, sun-dried tomatoes and capers and sauté for 3–4 minutes, or until the garlic is light golden. It is very important not to burn the garlic. Add the anchovy fillets and toss to coat in the hot oil.

Once the pasta is ready to go, use tongs to transfer it from the cooking water directly to the sauté pan. Add a ladleful of the starchy pasta water and toss the pasta continuously, until the anchovies are cooked and the pasta is evenly coated in the tomato and caper sauce. Add more pasta water if the sauce is looking a little dry.

Give the pasta a quick taste and add salt if needed. Garnish with a light sprinkle of oregano and a good drizzle of strong extra virgin olive oil. Serve immediately, while it is nice and hot.

Spinach & Chickpeas
Espinacas con Garbanzos

Here's a dish that feels like a bowl of health, especially when you've been travelling around Andalucía and have filled yourself up with fried tapas. If you've spent time in Seville, you've probably been offered this in tapas bars – it's another delicious example of the mosaic of cultures that is southern Spain. Though I had had it before, it was on a harvest trip to visit Marina Segura Gómez of Peña Luna near Málaga that this dish properly blew my mind and I knew it had to be in this book.

Serves 4

- 5 tablespoons extra virgin olive oil, plus extra for drizzling
- 10 blanched almonds
- 1 slice of day-old bread, crusts removed, then torn into pieces
- ½ onion, diced
- 3 garlic cloves, thinly sliced
- 1 tomato, diced
- 1 tablespoon tomato purée
- 2 teaspoons ground cumin
- 2 teaspoons smoked paprika
- 1 tablespoon sherry or red wine vinegar
- 200g (7oz) young leaf spinach
- 500g (1lb 2oz) cooked, canned or jarred chickpeas, drained
- salt and freshly ground black pepper
- bread, to serve

Heat 2 tablespoons of the EVOO in a medium-sized saucepan over a medium heat. Once hot, add the almonds and bread and fry until the bread is crisp and the almonds are toasted.

Add the onion and garlic and cook for about 5 minutes, until softened and starting to turn golden. Add the tomato, tomato purée, cumin and paprika, stir to combine and cook for another minute to mellow the spices.

Transfer this mixture to a blender or food processor, add the vinegar and blitz into a paste. Season with salt and pour a tablespoon of EVOO into the blender as it whizzes, until you have a smooth, spoonable consistency.

Heat the remaining 2 tablespoons EVOO in the saucepan over a medium heat. Throw in the spinach and chickpeas and cook until the leaves have wilted slightly. Add the mixture from the blender and stir to combine.

Scoop into shallow bowls, drizzle with EVOO and serve hot as tapas with bread (and spoons).

MAKE IT YOUR OWN
Add a squeeze of lemon juice for acidity.
A pinch of cayenne pepper is good for heat.

TIP
This keeps well in the fridge (it actually tastes better the next day) and is suitable for freezing.

EVOO TO PAIR
Cornicabra, Picual or anything from Andaluciá that's made well.

Spiced Corn on the Cob
with Herbs

When autumn rolls in, something in me just needs to make corn recipes. And when a new-harvest oil hits the table, these iconic flavours just sing together. I think most people imagine only buttered corn on the cob, but there's so much more that can be done. Inspired by my own Texas roots and the elote (street corn) options I used to enjoy from food stands all over Austin, I've come up with my own version – swapping the mayo and condiments for fresh, whole ingredients, such as tangy feta, chillies and a flavourful olive oil.

Serves 4

- **4 corn cobs in their leaves**
- **extra virgin olive oil, for grilling and drizzling**
- **3–5 tablespoons feta cheese, crumbled**
- **2 tablespoons chopped fresh coriander**
- **1 red chilli, deseeded and thinly sliced**
- **1 lime**
- **sea salt flakes**

Preheat the grill to medium-high, or place a ridged griddle pan over a medium heat, or have the barbecue coals hot and ready to cook.

Pop the cobs into a large pan of boiling water and cook for 3–5 minutes, until slightly softened.

Drain the corn and, when cool enough to handle, peel back the leaves. Remove the silky threads around the corn, then fold the leaves back and tie them together using one of the leaves to secure the bundle.

Brush the corn with a little EVOO and grill in your preferred way for 3–5 minutes, turning to cook evenly until nicely charred all over.

Place the cobs on a serving plate. Sprinkle with the feta, coriander and chilli. Drizzle with a healthy pour of EVOO.

Finely zest the lime over the corn and squeeze over the juice. Season with salt and serve straight away.

MAKE IT YOUR OWN
Top with grated Parmesan cheese or nutritional yeast flakes for some extra umami.
If you don't have anything fresh, add chilli heat by sprinkling with cayenne pepper or a Mexican spice mixture. Replace the coriander with other herbs, such as mint or basil.
A drizzle of honey would be an exciting addition!

TIP
A handy addition here from food stylist Annie Rigg is to use the husks as handles – functional and pleasing to look at.

EVOO TO PAIR
Choose varieties such as Hojiblanca, Cornicabra and Cobrançosa.

Green Pasta
with Red Pepper Salsa

'I'm a bit late to the party with this one,' says recipe creator and chef Kali Jago (@kalijago), 'but the rich savouriness of a pasta sauce made with cavolo nero and olive oil is so appealing that I had to make my own.' For extra nutritional value, Kali makes this delicious vegan dish with beans, and adds a red pepper salsa for a twist.

 Serves 4

- 200g (7oz) cavolo nero, stalks trimmed
- small bunch of flat leaf parsley
- 3 garlic cloves
- 350g (12oz) dried pasta, such as rigatoni
- 140ml (4½fl oz) extra virgin olive oil
- juice of 1 lemon
- 3 tablespoons nutritional yeast
- 400g (14oz) can or jar of cooked butter beans, rinsed and drained
- salt and freshly ground black pepper

FOR THE SALSA
- 4 tablespoons extra virgin olive oil
- 4 garlic cloves, crushed
- 2cm (¾in) piece of fresh root ginger, grated
- 400g (14oz) roasted red peppers, deseeded and diced (from a jar, if you wish)
- ½ teaspoon chipotle flakes
- pinch of salt

Start by making the salsa. Heat the EVOO in a frying pan over a medium heat. When hot, add the garlic and ginger and sauté for 30 seconds. Add the diced peppers, chipotle flakes and salt. Reduce the heat slightly and cook, stirring often, for about 10 minutes, until the flavours have combined and mellowed. Remove from the heat and set aside.

Bring a large pan of salted water to the boil. Add the cavolo nero, parsley (leaves and stalks) and garlic cloves, and blanch for 2 minutes. Using a slotted spoon, transfer these ingredients to a bowl of iced water to halt the cooking.

Return the saucepan to the heat and bring the water back to the boil. Add the pasta and cook until al dente.

Meanwhile, drain the cooled cavolo nero, parsley and garlic, then place in a blender. Add the EVOO, lemon juice and nutritional yeast, and season with salt and pepper. Blitz the mixture into a smooth green sauce.

When the pasta is ready, drain through a colander, reserving 250ml (9fl oz) of the cooking water. Return the pasta to the pan, add the green sauce and butter beans and mix to combine, adding enough of the reserved water so that the sauce coats the pasta.

Serve the pasta in bowls topped with the red pepper salsa.

EVOO TO PAIR
An earlier harvest with green notes. Think Istria, Tuscany or Koroneiki.

Asparagus
with Burrata & Gremolata

Gremolata is essentially an Italian condiment, and one made from the season's best herbs is the perfect accompaniment to delicious burrata over asparagus. Although this takes only minutes to make, it is an indulgent starter or an easy lunch – a nice dish to have in your back pocket, so to speak.

Serves 2

- 1–2 tablespoons chopped mint or flat leaf parsley
- finely grated zest of 1 unwaxed lemon
- 1 garlic clove, crushed
- 10–12 asparagus spears, ends trimmed
- 2 tablespoons extra virgin olive oil, plus extra to serve
- 1 tablespoon balsamic vinegar, plus extra to serve
- 1 ball of burrata, about 150g (5½oz)
- salt and freshly ground black pepper

To make the gremolata, combine the mint, lemon zest and garlic in a small bowl.

Place a ridged griddle pan over a high heat until very hot. Meanwhile, drizzle the asparagus with the EVOO and vinegar and season with salt and pepper. Place the spears in the hot pan in a single layer and cook for 2–4 minutes, until tender and starting to char.

Arrange the asparagus on a platter, place the burrata on top and spoon over the gremolata. Drizzle with EVOO and balsamic vinegar and serve immediately.

MAKE IT YOUR OWN
Grill the asparagus on a barbecue or under the grill, or even roast it in a hot oven.
Pep up the gremolata with some sliced fresh red chilli.
Pistachios or pine nuts could be added for crunch.
Try different herb combos (basil and parsley, for example) or go full chimichurri and add some oregano.

TIP
The leftover pool of oil on the plate is essentially a loaded EVOO, so overload on the herbs, oil and lemon and mop up it all up with bread at the end.

EVOO TO PAIR
Croatian varieties work well here, as do options like Galega and Leccino.

Pasta con le Sarde

As they say in Sicily, Palermo is closer to Tunis than Rome. The island has a distinctive connection to North Africa and this dish showcases that. I first ordered it at a restaurant in Cefalù because of how interesting it sounded, but weeks later I found myself still craving these flavours – the salty-sweet combination of sardines and raisins is a surprising delight. On every trip back, I find myself with this on my plate, learning the nuances of this classic Sicilian dish as I update my home recipe...

Serves 4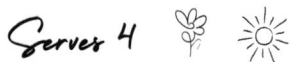

- 40g (1½oz) pine nuts
- 100ml (3½fl oz) extra virgin olive oil, plus extra to serve
- 75g (2¾oz) fresh breadcrumbs (sourdough or ciabatta are ideal)
- 100ml (3½fl oz) white wine
- pinch of saffron threads
- 350g (12oz) bucatini or spaghetti
- 1 small onion, finely chopped
- 1 small fennel bulb, finely chopped, fronds reserved
- 3 anchovy fillets
- 2 garlic cloves, crushed
- 2 x 200g (7oz) cans sardines in oil
- 40g (1½oz) raisins or sultanas
- finely grated zest and juice of 1 unwaxed lemon

MAKE IT YOUR OWN
Add chilli flakes for heat and chard or spinach for greens.
You can skip the breadcrumbs and just use Parmesan if it's easier.

EVOO TO PAIR
Cerasuola, Nocellara de Belice, Tonda Iblea, early harvest Picual.

Place a large frying pan over a medium heat. When hot, add the pine nuts and toast for about 2 minutes, shaking the pan so that they colour evenly. When golden, transfer to a plate and set aside.

Add 2 tablespoons of the oil to the pan, tip in the breadcrumbs and fry until crisp and golden, stirring often. Transfer to a plate and set aside. Wipe the pan clean with kitchen paper.

Pour the wine into a small bowl, add the saffron and leave it to soak for a minute.

Bring a large pan of salted water to the boil and cook the pasta until al dente – 'for no more than 8 minutes' according to Francesca Oliva, our Sicilian producer.

Meanwhile, heat another 2 tablespoons oil in the frying pan, add the onion and cook for 1 minute. Add the chopped fennel, anchovies and garlic and cook for 5 minutes, mashing the anchovies with the back of a spoon until they have 'melted'. By this time the onion and fennel will have softened too.

Break the sardines into large chunks and add to the pan along with the saffron-infused wine and the raisins. Bring to the boil and allow the sauce to bubble and reduce slightly.

Using tongs, transfer the cooked pasta from the water directly into the frying pan and combine with the sardine mixture. Toss in the pine nuts, lemon juice to taste and stir in 75–100ml (2½–3½fl oz) pasta water if the sauce is looking dry.

Serve the pasta in bowls with a sprinkling of breadcrumbs, the reserved fennel fronds, some freshly grated lemon zest and a healthy drizzle of olive oil.

Roasted Beetroot & Burrata

We all have a friend who just seems to 'get' food. From baking bread with their own starter to making their own confit – it's as if nothing in the kitchen is too difficult for them to manage. My lovely friend Aurore is one such person. Maybe it's the fact that she comes from a French family of foodies. Maybe it's from her years of working with the Slow Food movement. Or maybe it's just her natural creativity that makes pairing flavours and coming up with interesting recipes seem so easy. She shared this recipe using our Greek oil when we first launched, and it was just the perfect winter salad.

Serves 2-4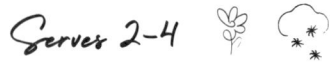

- 4 raw beetroot, each about the size of a satsuma
- 4–5 tablespoons extra virgin olive oil
- 50g (1¾oz) walnut halves
- 1 ball of burrata, about 150g (5½oz)
- bitter leaves, such as radicchio (Castelfranco), or rocket
- sea salt flakes and freshly ground black pepper

Preheat the oven to 180°C (160°C fan/350°F/Gas mark 4).

Cut the beetroot into quarters or sixths, depending on size; there is no need to peel them. Tip them into a small roasting tray and add 2 tablespoons of the EVOO and a pinch of salt. Roast for 20–30 minutes, or until tender and cooked through when tested with the point of a sharp knife.

While the beetroot are roasting, tip the walnuts into another tray and toast in the oven for about 5 minutes, until crisp.

Remove the beetroot and walnuts from the oven and leave to cool for 10–15 minutes.

Arrange the beetroot and bitter leaves on a serving dish with the burrata. Crush the walnuts in your hands and scatter them over the salad. Drizzle with the remaining 2–3 tablespoons of EVOO, then season with a good pinch of salt and some freshly ground pepper to serve.

MAKE IT YOUR OWN
Drizzle with a little balsamic vinegar and sprinkle with a small handful of chopped soft herbs, such as chives.

EVOO TO PAIR
Delicate like Biancollila, Leccino or Manaki. Nutty notes of a slightly later harvest.

Capatouille

The Italians have caponata, the French have ratatouille: this takes the best of both to create capatouille! Salty, fresh, a little bit spicy and smoky, this is the dish that summer produce is made for. The key is in quality ingredients, so find the best tomatoes, aubergines and courgettes you can. Easy to scale up or down, and good as a main course or a side dish (to baked fish, for example), it's the brainchild of our team member Frides O'Neill, who's the mind behind many of our iconic serves.

 Serves 6

- 2 onions, diced
- 4 tablespoons extra virgin olive oil, plus extra for drizzling
- 4 garlic cloves, crushed
- 1 teaspoon dried oregano
- 1 teaspoon smoked paprika
- ½ teaspoon Aleppo pepper
- 400g (14oz) can chopped tomatoes
- 150g (5½oz) cherry tomatoes, halved
- 3 carrots, coarsely grated
- 20g (¾oz) capers
- ½ small bunch basil, leaves chopped
- 4 slender aubergines, sliced 1cm (½in) thick
- 4 courgettes, sliced 1cm (½in) thick
- 4–6 large tomatoes, sliced 1cm (½in) thick
- sea salt flakes and black pepper
- crusty bread, to serve

Place the onions in a large saucepan, add the EVOO and a generous pinch of salt, and cook over a low–medium heat for about 10 minutes, stirring often until translucent and soft. Add the garlic and sweat for another 2–3 minutes.

Increase the heat, add the oregano, smoked paprika and Aleppo pepper, and allow to sizzle for 30 seconds.

Add the chopped tomatoes, cherry tomatoes and grated carrots, and cook over a low heat for about 30 minutes, stirring occasionally, until the carrots are soft and the tomatoes break down into a rich sauce.

Add the capers and basil, and season to taste with salt and black pepper.

Preheat the oven to 180°C (160°C fan/350°F/Gas mark 4).

Spoon the sauce into an ovenproof dish – a round dish is nice to reflect the shape of the aubergines, courgettes and tomatoes that you now arrange alternately on top in neat concentric circles overlapping each other.

Sprinkle with sea salt flakes and 1 teaspoon crushed black pepper and drizzle generously with EVOO. Bake for 30 minutes, until golden and bubbling. Serve with crusty bread.

MAKE IT YOUR OWN
If serving this as a main course, make it richer by adding a sprinkling of feta, mozzarella or Parmesan on the top for the last 10 minutes of baking. Rather than alternating the vegetable slices for the topping, you could arrange each type in its own concentric rings.

TIP
Always make more than you need, as any leftovers can be blended to create a delicious pasta sauce.

EVOO TO PAIR
Something punchier like Nocellara, Coratina, Cornicabra or Koroneiki.

Courgette Noodles
with Prawn & Cherry Tomatoes

'This is an incredibly easy, light and summery recipe, especially good if you can get your hands on some fresh prawns,' says Lena Puhar O'Grady of Brist Olive Oil in Croatia. 'It's the perfect Mediterranean dinner for me on a hot summer evening with a glass of dry Malvasia wine.'

Serves 4

- 400g (14oz) peeled prawns, deveined and rinsed
- 3 tablespoons extra virgin olive oil, plus extra to serve
- 2 garlic cloves, thinly sliced or crushed
- 100g (3½oz) cherry tomatoes
- 100ml (3½fl oz) white wine
- 500g (1lb 2oz) courgettes, sliced into thin noodles (see Tips)
- leaves from 1 sprig of thyme

Dry the prawns on kitchen paper.

Pour the EVOO into a large pan, add the garlic and cook for 30 seconds over a medium heat. Add the prawns and sauté for a couple of minutes, until just cooked through.

Add the tomatoes and wine and continue to cook until the liquid has completely evaporated.

Add the courgette noodles, increase the heat slightly and cook for another 1–2 minutes, until they are just softened.

Divide between plates, scatter with the thyme leaves and serve with a generous drizzle of EVOO.

MAKE IT YOUR OWN
Try adding a pinch of crushed dried chilli flakes and a little lemon zest, and serve with a squeeze of lemon.

TIPS
You don't need a spiralizer to cut courgettes into thin noodles. You can use a mandoline, julienne peeler or just a sharp knife.
It's easy to overcook courgette noodles, so test them regularly until al dente and still vibrant green.

EVOO TO PAIR
Choose a grassy oil with green notes.

Vania's Pasta
with Creamed Cauliflower

'Pasta cu li vrocculi arriminati' is a traditional first course of Sicilian cuisine that our producer Vania Sarullo's family has been making for generations near Agrigento. It bears traces of the island's slightly baroque opulence of the past, as it contains saffron, pine nuts and raisins. Like Pasta con le Sarde (see page 119), this is a dish that tells a story of Sicily's layers of influence.

Serves 4

- 50g (1¾oz) raisins
- generous pinch of saffron threads
- 1 large Romanesco cauliflower, or regular white cauliflower
- 350g (12oz) bucatini
- 3 tablespoons extra virgin olive oil, plus extra to serve
- 1 onion, finely chopped
- 1 large garlic clove, crushed
- 3 anchovies in olive oil, drained
- 50g (1¾oz) pine nuts, toasted
- 3 tablespoons grated Pecorino cheese, plus extra to serve
- salt and freshly ground black pepper

MAKE IT YOUR OWN
Add a spoonful of tomato purée for a bit more tang.
To make this a more substantial meal, serve with greens. Adding beans or Italian sausage also works nicely.

EVOO TO PAIR
Sicilian cultivars like Biancolilla, Tonda Iblea, Nocellara.

Put the raisins to soak in a bowl of hot water to plump them up. In another small bowl, soak the saffron in 1 tablespoon hot water. Set both aside.

Trim the cauliflower and cut into florets. Bring a large pan of salted water to the boil, add the cauliflower and cook for about 8 minutes, until tender. Using a slotted spoon, transfer the florets to a bowl of cold water.

Return the cauliflower cooking water to the heat and bring to the boil. Add the bucatini and cook until al dente.

Meanwhile, warm the EVOO in a sauté pan, add the onion and cook over a medium heat, stirring often, until soft and just starting to caramelize. Add the garlic and anchovies and cook for another minute, until the anchovies have melted.

Add the saffron and its soaking water to the onion mixture, cover with a lid and continue cooking for another minute or so.

Drain the cauliflower florets, add to the sauté pan and stir to combine. Drain the raisins and add to the pan along with the pine nuts and a pinch of salt. Cook over a low–medium heat for another 3 minutes, until the cauliflower has heated through and broken down into small pieces.

Using tongs or a slotted spoon, transfer the pasta to the cauliflower sauce, then add a ladleful of the pasta water and the cheese. Stir to combine.

Serve in bowls with extra grated Pecorino and a drizzle of EVOO.

Greek Horta

Boiled Wild Greens

If you spend any time with a Greek family, especially in the countryside, you'll quickly get introduced to the ritual of foraging, boiling and dressing wild greens. Known as horta, these bitter greens are a beloved staple. Whether dandelion, amaranth, chicory or some other edible leaves are gathered, they all get washed, boiled and bathed in olive oil and lemon juice. It's a simple, nourishing and strangely addictive dish. This recipe is a true winter healer. It's packed with folate, magnesium and all sorts of phytonutrients from the greens, along with antioxidants from the EVOO. All these aid in blood sugar regulation, digestion and combating inflammation. It's also something anyone can eat, so brilliant to serve as a side when having people around. Most of us don't get enough greens, and this is such a simple, delicious way to do that!

 Serves 4

- large bunch (about 450g/1lb) of greens, such as spinach, chard, chicory or kale
- juice of 1 lemon
- generous glug of extra virgin olive oil
- salt and freshly ground black pepper

Start by thoroughly washing the greens in cold running water. Very roughly chop the leaves, giving just a couple of chops to break up large pieces; you don't want the greens too fine or too small.

Bring a large pan of salted water to the boil. Add the greens and boil for 5–10 minutes, until tender, but still vibrant green. The cooking time will depend on what type of greens you are using.

Use a slotted spoon to transfer the greens to a serving bowl, bringing a bit of the cooking liquid with you as you go.

Douse liberally with lemon juice and extra virgin olive oil, season with sea salt and black pepper and then toss well. Serve immediately.

MAKE IT YOUR OWN
Try adding a crushed garlic clove or sliced chillies for an extra kick. Horta is traditionally made with whatever greens are growing in the fields at the time of foraging. Whatever is seasonal is the best. It's also nice to use a combination of greens for extra texture and taste.

TIP
The cooking liquid is packed with nutrients and commonly referred to as tiger's milk, so don't waste it. Do as the Greeks, and drink it up at the end.

EVOO TO PAIR
Choose Koroneiki or Tsounati for Greek authenticity; or a buttery Arbequina if you want to mellow the bitterness of the leaves.

Elena's Catalan Spinach
with Currants & Pine Nuts

Espinacas a la Catalana is a classic Catalan dish that combines greens with nuts and fruit for that incredible sweet and savoury balance that weaves through so much of Mediterranean cuisine. This recipe is shared with us by Elena Gracia, who's originally from Barcelona. She's been working in olive oil for a decade to get the best of small-scale Spanish producers, particularly from her home region, into farmers' markets in the UK.

Serves 4

- 2 large bunches of spinach (about 400g/14oz in total)
- 4 tablespoons extra virgin olive oil, plus extra for drizzling
- 2 garlic cloves, thinly sliced
- 3 tablespoons pine nuts
- 3 tablespoons currants or raisins
- 4 slices of day-old bread, such as sourdough
- salt and freshly ground black pepper

Trim any tough stems from the spinach and wash the leaves well under cold running water to remove any grit. Place them in a large pan with just the water clinging to them, cover and steam for about 2 minutes, until just wilted. Drain in a colander. When cool enough to handle, gently squeeze any excess water out of the leaves.

Pour the EVOO into a large frying pan over a medium heat. When hot, add the garlic and sauté gently for 1–2 minutes, until just golden. Add the pine nuts and currants and cook for another minute or so, until the nuts are golden.

Add the drained spinach and stir everything together until the greens are glossy and well coated in the garlicky oil. Season with salt and pepper.

Toast the bread either under a grill or on a hot ridged griddle pan. Drizzle with a little more EVOO and serve alongside the spinach.

MAKE IT YOUR OWN
Take this dish the extra mile by adding some fried bacon bits or chopped Spanish jamón.

EVOO TO PAIR
Catalan varieties like Arbequina, Morruda or Empeltre.

Family Feasting

'It is a long and laborious process,
which does not simply appear in a bottle;
there is a whole year of hard work behind it.'

—Ana Cardoso, producer and miller, Tratturo de Fronteira, Alentejo, Portugal

Maria's Spanakopita
Spinach & Feta Pie

'Guys, have you eaten?' These are words we regularly hear on our visits to Maria Amargiotaki, our family friend and first producer in Crete. It doesn't matter what the response is because food is probably already in the works. One day, although we were all working, including her, she casually whipped up one of my favourite Greek dishes. Maria is an expert with spanakopita: I've watched her gracefully layer it together while children create chaos around her and too many of us are crowded into her kitchen. The secret to making this iconic Greek dish is layers and layers of filo pastry plus lashings of EVOO. This light, flaky and crunchy source of goodness could be the perfect replacement for your favourite hearty winter pies. Just get ready to layer up!

Serves 4–6

- 6–8 tablespoons extra virgin olive oil
- 1 onion, finely chopped
- 1 bunch of spring onions, trimmed and thinly sliced
- 2 garlic cloves, crushed
- small bunch of dill, chopped
- 800g (1lb 12oz) spinach, washed and roughly chopped
- 12 large sheets of filo pastry (packets vary, so check the contents)
- 200g (7oz) feta cheese
- salt and freshly ground black pepper

Heat 2 tablespoons of the EVOO in a large sauté pan or saucepan over a medium heat. When hot, add the onion and cook for 2 minutes, stirring often until it starts to soften.

Add the spring onions and garlic and cook for 2 minutes more, then add the chopped dill and cook for another minute. Finally, add the spinach, lower the heat and cook for 10–15 minutes, until it has softened and wilted. (There is no need to add water as the drops clinging to the spinach are enough.)

Tip the spinach into a sieve over a bowl and press down on the mixture with the back of a spoon to remove excess oil and water. Leave to cool for 30 minutes.

Preheat the oven to 180°C (160°C fan/350°F/Gas mark 4). Brush the inside of a 33 x 25cm (13 x 10in) baking tin with EVOO.

Carefully unroll the filo pastry sheets. Brush the first sheet with EVOO, then lay it in the prepared tin, covering the base and sides and allowing the excess pastry to drape over the sides. Brush the next sheet of filo with EVOO and place on top of the first. Continue this layering until you have 6 layers of pastry in the tin.

Now it's time to add the spinach. If it is still very wet, squeeze it between your hands to remove more moisture, or it will make

MAKE IT YOUR OWN
The recipe works with different greens, depending on what's in season.

TIP
Keep the spinach cooking water, as it can be stored for adding to stock when cooking a risotto.

EVOO TO PAIR
Grassy notes like Koroneiki.

the pastry too wet to become crisp and crunchy. Season well with pepper, but go easy on the salt as the feta is already salty.

Spread the spinach over the pastry-lined tin in an even layer and crumble the feta over the top.

Brush another sheet of filo with oil and place it over the filling. Continue oiling and layering the pastry until the remaining sheets are used up.

Trim off the overhanging pastry, then brush the top with EVOO and bake for 40–60 minutes, until the pie is crisp and golden brown. Serve hot or room temperature.

Cauliflower Caponata

Caponata, a Sicilian vegetable stew, is a masterclass in balancing sweet, sour and salty. It's most often made with aubergine, which you first fry in lots of olive oil, perhaps making it less of a weeknight situation. This buttery cauliflower version is all done in the oven and to Anna Jones, the celebrated British food writer, is just as good as the aubergine version. It has the texture of a stew and can be eaten warm as an antipasto, as is most common in Italy, or on toast or tossed through pasta. This is a recipe of Anna's, which she kindly shared with our community.

Serves 4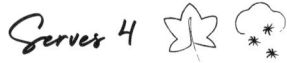

- **1 large cauliflower, cut into 4cm (1½in) florets**
- **3 red onions, each cut into 6 or 8 wedges**
- **3 celery sticks, sliced into 3cm (1¼in) chunks**
- **3 tablespoons extra virgin olive oil, plus extra to serve**
- **2 tablespoons white wine vinegar**
- **2 x 400g (14oz) cans plum tomatoes**
- **100g (3½oz) black or green pitted olives**
- **50g (1¾oz) capers**
- **50g (1¾oz) raisins**
- **½ bunch of flat leaf parsley, leaves roughly chopped**
- **salt and freshly ground black pepper**
- **warm crusty bread, to serve**

Preheat the oven to 200°C (180°C fan/400°F/Gas mark 6).

Spread out the cauliflower, onions and celery in a large roasting tray. Drizzle with the EVOO and 1 tablespoon white wine vinegar, and season with salt and pepper. Toss to coat, then roast for 25 minutes, until everything is slightly charred and starting to soften. Turn the oven down to 180°C (160°C fan/350°F/Gas mark 4) and remove the tray.

Add the tomatoes to the vegetables, crushing them in your hands or with a spoon as you go. Add the olives, capers and raisins. Stir well, then return the tray to the oven for a further 40 minutes, or until the mixture is soft and sticky.

Remove the tray and stir in the remaining tablespoon of vinegar and the chopped parsley. Finish with a very generous drizzle of EVOO to bring it all together and serve with warm crusty bread.

EVOO TO PAIR
More intense varieties like from Puglia, Sicily, or Tuscany work well.

Cretan Dolmades

Dolmades, or stuffed vine leaves, are part of a family of leaf wraps filled with vegetables, herbs, rice and sometimes meat. They are widely made in the eastern Mediterranean, so there are many varieties and differences in the local ingredients used, but most are based around vine leaves, rice, lemon and olive oil. It took Maria no time to catch on that these were my absolute favourite of the dishes she served, so they've become a staple during my visits to her olive groves in Crete. Maria is famous in the family for how neatly and quickly she can make multiple servings of dolmades. While I've come to appreciate the seasonal differences you can make to them, this recipe of Maria's is still my favourite. Ideally, use vine leaves canned in brine, but boiled cabbage leaves can be used if you prefer.

Makes 65-70

- 200g (7oz) short-grain rice (as used for paella or risotto)
- small bunch of flat leaf parsley, finely chopped
- 1 onion, finely chopped
- 2 tomatoes, skinned and finely chopped
- 1 small courgette, coarsely grated
- 1 small potato, peeled and coarsely grated
- juice of 1 lemon
- 70 vine leaves canned in brine (150–200g/4½–7oz), rinsed under cold water
- 125ml (5fl oz) extra virgin olive oil, plus extra to serve
- 125ml (4fl oz) passata (optional – it depends how red you want your filling to be)
- salt and freshly ground black pepper
- Greek yogurt, to serve

Mix the uncooked rice, parsley, onion, tomatoes, courgette, potato and lemon juice in a bowl and season well with salt and pepper.

Lay out a single vine leaf, underside uppermost, so it appears heart-shaped, with the point at the bottom.

Put a teaspoon of the rice mixture in the middle of the leaf, then fold one arch of the heart over it. Repeat with the other arch. As you do this, you might need to squish the rice so it's held tight in the centre.

Fold the leaves in from the side to encase the filling and roll down to the point; the rice should stay snug in the middle of the parcel and remain closed during cooking. Place the parcel, seam-side down, in a deep, heavy-based casserole dish about 20–23cm (8–9in) wide. Continue until you have filled all the vine leaves, packing them in neat, tight layers as you go. The number of layers will depend on the size of your dish.

Pour in the olive oil, passata (if using), and enough cold water to cover the dolmades by 2–3cm (¾–1¼in).

Place a plate on top of the dolmades to keep them in place and prevent them opening as they cook. Maria also places a cup on top of the plate to ensure the dolmades stay put.

Cover with a lid, place the dish over a low–medium heat and bring to the boil. Immediately lower the heat to a simmer

MAKE IT YOUR OWN

You can leave out the potato and tomatoes and use dill instead of parsley.

EVOO TO PAIR

Kalamon or Koroneiki, Tsounanti, Hojiblanca.

– or, as Maria says, 'half the heat of the boil' – and cook for 15–20 minutes.

Now, she notes, 'the most important thing is that after they are cooked and taken off the fire, you don't remove any water. You simply lift out the cup and plate and within 5 minutes the water has disappeared!'

You can keep the dolmades warm in the dish for serving, or leave them to cool, then batch them up for the fridge, where they will keep well for a couple of days. Dolmades are great to make the day before you have people over, as they can be prepared and cooked ahead and served at any temperature.

Serve with a dollop of Greek yogurt and a drizzle of EVOO.

Rustic Mediterranean Olive Bread

This hearty loaf is another recipe from Claudia Hanna. Her family comes from across the Middle East and the time she has spent guiding people through the food markets of the Eastern Levant has helped her create recipes like this one. While this type of bread would originally have been made using olives with stones in them, this version is easier to share with your guests and to use for toast or a sandwich.

Serves 6

- 450g (1lb) strong flour
- 50g (1¾oz) strong wholemeal flour
- 7g sachet fast-action dried yeast
- 1 teaspoon salt
- 300ml (½ pint) lukewarm water
- 6 tablespoons extra virgin olive oil, plus extra for greasing
- 125g (4½oz) pitted black olives, sliced
- small bunch of flat leaf parsley or coriander, chopped
- 3 spring onions, trimmed and thinly sliced

MAKE IT YOUR OWN
You can use any type of olives, but Claudia thinks those with stones taste richer. If you buy this type, remove the stones before baking.

TIP
A finely chopped onion can be used in place of spring onions.

EVOO TO PAIR
Levant styles like Kypriaki, Gemlik, Souri or the classic Koroneiki.

Tip both flours into the bowl of a stand mixer fitted with a dough hook. Add the yeast and salt and mix to combine. Add the warm water and 4 tablespoons of the EVOO and mix at a slow speed until combined. Scrape down the sides of the bowl and continue mixing at a medium speed for about 8 minutes, until the dough is smooth and elastic.

Turn the dough out of the bowl and shape into a ball. Lightly oil the bowl, return the dough to it, then cover and leave to rise at room temperature for about 1 hour, or until doubled in size.

Add the olives, herbs and spring onions to the dough and mix them in using your hands.

Transfer the dough to a large, oiled baking tray, drizzle with 2 tablespoons EVOO, then use your hands to flatten the dough to a thickness of about 3cm (1¼in). The olive oil will give the baked loaf a beautiful, glossy brown crust.

Loosely cover the dough and leave to rise again for 45 minutes.

Preheat the oven to 220°C (200°C fan/425°F/Gas mark 7), then bake the loaf for about 30 minutes, or until golden brown and well risen. Serve warm.

Portuguese Baked Cod
Bacalhau à Lagareiro

While this dish requires some advance planning (the salt cod needs to soak for at least 24 hours), it's well worth it. And seeing as the Portuguese name translates to 'cod of the olive oil mill worker' (lagareiro), this recipe had to be included in a book about olive oil. This dish comes from Portugal's olive regions and was a way to best showcase the new-harvest EVOO – in the place where it was made, by the people who made it. This version was shared with us by our lovely producer Ana Cardoso in Alentejo, and while it can be made year-round, it's definitely one to try with a fresh oil just after harvest.

Serves 4

- 600–800g (1lb 7oz–1lb 12oz) salt cod, cut into 4 pieces
- 1kg (2lb 4oz) small new potatoes
- 4–5 tablespoons extra virgin olive oil
- leaves from 1 sprig of rosemary
- 2 onions, sliced
- 4 garlic cloves, sliced
- sea salt flakes and freshly ground black pepper

Rinse the cod under cold running water, then place in a large bowl or plastic container and cover with double the volume of cold water. Cover and place in the fridge. Leave to soak for 24–48 hours, changing the water every 8 hours or so. The soaking time depends on the thickness of the fish.

Preheat the oven to 200°C (180°C fan/400°F/Gas mark 6).

Place the whole unpeeled potatoes in a roasting tray and toss with 2 tablespoons of the EVOO. Add the rosemary and season with sea salt flakes. Roast for about 30 minutes, until tender.

Drain the cod and rinse under cold water. Place in a sauté pan, cover with water and bring to a simmer. Continue simmering for 5 minutes, then lift out the fish and pat dry on kitchen paper.

Meanwhile, pour 2–3 tablespoons of the remaining EVOO into a frying pan and place over a medium heat. Add the onions and garlic and cook for about 10 minutes, until starting to soften and caramelize at the edges.

Remove the potatoes from the oven and use a fish slice to lightly crush them and break the skin. Move them to one side of the tray and place the cod in the space. Spoon the onions and garlic on top, together with their delicious cooking oil.

Return to the oven for a further 15 minutes, or until the potatoes and onions are crisp and the fish is cooked through.

MAKE IT YOUR OWN
Sprinkle with chopped parsley and a few olives as a garnish.

EVOO TO PAIR
Galega, Cobrançosa, Cornicabra.

Meat & Pasta Casserole

Giouvetsi

Giouvetsi (or youvetsi) is the kind of slow-simmered comfort dish you want to gather around on a cold day. This version, made with love and plenty of red wine, comes to us, once again, from our beloved friend Maria Amargiotaki in Crete. It's classic, rustic and ideal for a family Sunday lunch. The kritharaki (orzo-style pasta) soaks up all the rich flavours from the veal, tomato and spices, creating a dish that's hearty but never heavy. Don't skip the crumbled feta on top – it brings everything to life.

Serves 4–6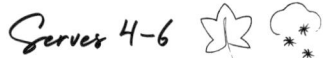

- **600g (1lb 5oz) veal shoulder, cut into 2–3cm (¾–1¼in) chunks**
- **3 tablespoons extra virgin olive oil, plus extra for drizzling**
- **2 large onions, finely chopped**
- **2 garlic cloves, crushed**
- **4 large ripe tomatoes or 400g (14oz) can chopped tomatoes**
- **½ –1 teaspoon ground cumin**
- **1 rounded tablespoon tomato purée**
- **250ml (9fl oz) red wine**
- **leaves from 1 sprig of thyme**
- **1 bay leaf**
- **1 cinnamon stick**
- **1 teaspoon sugar or honey**
- **500ml (18fl oz) beef stock or water**
- **250g (9oz) kritharaki pasta (if you can find it), or orzo**
- **salt and freshly ground black pepper**
- **crumbled feta cheese, to serve**

EVOO TO PAIR
Koroneiki or any rich, peppery variety to stand up to the wine and tomato base.

Season the meat with salt and pepper. Heat 2 tablespoons of the EVOO in a sauté pan over a high heat and cook the veal in batches until browned on all sides. Transfer to a flameproof casserole dish.

Add the onions to the sauté pan, reduce the heat to medium and cook for about 8 minutes, until softened and just starting to colour. Add the garlic and cook for a minute more.

Meanwhile, if using fresh tomatoes, either coarsely grate or roughly chop them, then transfer to a blender or food processor and blitz into 1cm (½in) pieces. Otherwise, open the can.

Add the cumin and tomato purée to the onions and cook for another minute, stirring continuously, until the purée is slightly caramelized.

Pour the wine into the pan, stirring to loosen any bits stuck to the bottom, and allow to bubble for about 1 minute to burn off the alcohol. Add the thyme, bay leaf, cinnamon stick, sugar and chopped tomatoes, then stir and cook for 3–4 minutes.

Pour the tomato mixture into the casserole dish and add just enough stock to cover the meat. Place over a low heat, cover with a lid and simmer gently for about 1 hour 20 minutes, or until the meat is tender. Maria uses a pressure cooker, in which the meat cooks in about 35 minutes, but it can also be braised for about 1½ hours in an oven preheated to 140°C (120°C fan/275°F/Gas mark 1). Taste the sauce and add salt, pepper or extra sugar, as needed.

MAKE IT YOUR OWN
The veal can be swapped for chopped lamb shoulder or braising steak, depending on your preference or what's available.

TIP
Maria suggests tucking some of the meat into the pasta to avoid burning, though 'a little bit burnt' actually tastes good!

Preheat the oven to 180°C (160°C fan/350°F/Gas mark 4).

Heat the remaining tablespoon EVOO in a large frying pan over a medium heat, add the pasta and very lightly toast for 1 minute, stirring continuously. Add this to the veal mixture, stir to combine, then add the remaining stock. The liquid should cover the meat and pasta by 2–3cm (¾–1¼in), so add water if necessary. Stir well, cover loosely with foil and place in the oven for about 15 minutes, until the pasta is al dente.

Set the dish aside to rest for 3–4 minutes, then serve with crumbled feta on top and a drizzle of EVOO.

Maria's Moussaka

This insanely delicious recipe is another dish from a harvest lunch with the Amargiotakis family in Crete – one we still dream about it to this day. We sat on the ground, surrounded by olive trees, and it was the best moussaka we've ever had. It goes to show that the best food isn't necessarily served on white tablecloths in fancy restaurants. This hearty dish might be considered winter food, but aubergine season is summer and autumn, so make this while they're at their best.

Serves 6–8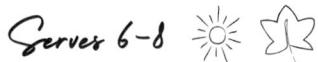

- 5 aubergines
- about 8 tablespoons extra virgin olive oil
- 5 large, waxy potatoes
- 2 large onions, finely chopped
- 3 fat garlic cloves, crushed
- 1kg (2lb 4oz) minced pork or veal
- 1 tablespoon ground cumin
- ½ teaspoon ground allspice
- pinch of ground cinnamon
- pinch of freshly grated nutmeg
- 2 tablespoons tomato purée
- 250ml (9fl oz) red or white wine
- 2 x 400g (14oz) cans chopped tomatoes
- 2 teaspoons dried oregano
- 1 bay leaf
- salt and freshly ground black pepper

TIP
Frying not your thing? Feel free to roast your potatoes in the oven in a generous smothering of EVOO and a bit of salt.

EVOO TO PAIR
Koroneiki, Kalamon, Halkidiki, Tsounati.

Preheat the oven to 220°C (200°C fan/425°F/Gas mark 7).

Trim the aubergines and slice into rounds 1cm (½in) thick. Brush the slices with a little EVOO, sprinkle with salt and arrange in a single layer on 2–3 baking trays. Bake for 25 minutes, until golden, then set aside.

Meanwhile, peel the potatoes and cut into slices 5mm (¼in) thick. Pour 2 tablespoons olive oil into a large frying pan over a medium heat. When hot, add a single layer of sliced potatoes and fry until golden and soft. Transfer to a tray and continue to fry the potatoes in batches, adding more oil as needed.

Wipe out the pan with kitchen paper, add 2–3 tablespoons olive oil and warm over a low–medium heat. Add the onions to the pan and sweat for about 10 minutes, until soft. Add the garlic and cook for a further minute. Increase the heat to medium, add the meat and continue to cook, stirring often, until it has browned.

Add the spices to the pan, stir well and cook for a minute before adding the tomato purée. Stir well, cook for a minute, then add the wine. Allow most of the wine to evaporate before adding the tomatoes, oregano and bay leaf. Season well with salt and pepper, then stir and reduce the heat to low. Half-cover the pan and allow to simmer for 45 minutes, until the sauce has thickened and most of the liquid has evaporated.

Onto the béchamel sauce. Melt the butter in another pan over a low–medium heat. Stir in the flour and cook for a minute until it resembles a paste. Slowly add the milk, whisking continuously until smooth.

Bring to the boil while stirring, then reduce the heat and simmer for 3–4 minutes, until the sauce resembles thick cream. Remove the pan from the heat, add the egg yolks, three-quarters of the cheese and season with salt and the freshly grated nutmeg.

Assemble your moussaka in a large baking dish, roughly 35 x 25cm (14 x 10in), in this order: first arrange the potatoes in a neat layer, followed by half the aubergines. Add all the meat filling, then the remaining aubergines. Cover with the béchamel sauce, sprinkle with the remaining cheese and grate over a little nutmeg. You can now either chill the moussaka until required, or preheat the oven to 180°C (160°C fan/350°F/Gas mark 4).

Bake the moussaka for about 1 hour, until the top layer is golden and the filling piping hot. Leave to rest for 5 minutes before serving.

FOR THE BÉCHAMEL SAUCE

- **75g (2¾oz) butter**
- **90g (3¼oz) plain flour**
- **900ml (1½ pints) milk**
- **2 egg yolks**
- **150g (5½oz) Kefalotyri cheese, or Parmesan, or mature Cheddar, grated**
- **pinch of freshly grated nutmeg**

Stuffed Peppers & Tomatoes
Yemista

A classic dish that you'll find in homes and tavernas across Cyprus and Greece, with roots deep into the Middle East and across North Africa, Turkey and the Balkans. This version comes to us from Christina Soteriou, a Cypriot chef and vegan cookbook author who specializes in plant-forward vibracy from the Levant.

Serves 5–6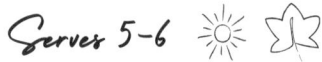

- 1 onion, finely chopped
- 5 garlic cloves, crushed
- 1 courgette, coarsely grated
- 2 tablespoons tomato purée
- 4–6 tablespoons extra virgin olive oil
- 150g (5½oz) short-grain rice
- 400g (14oz) can chopped tomatoes
- 600ml (20fl oz) vegetable stock
- 30g (1oz) pine nuts, toasted
- 1 teaspoon dried oregano
- 1 tablespoon mint leaves, torn
- 3 large tomatoes
- 3 red or orange peppers
- 500g (1lb 2oz) baking potatoes
- 2 tablespoons chopped flat leaf parsley
- salt and freshly ground black pepper

MAKE IT YOUR OWN
Although this is a vegan recipe, Marianna, our producer in the Peloponnese, says that it is also often made with minced meat and topped with feta cheese. 'The stuffed tomatoes without mince are called "orphans"!' She also adds raisins to her recipe when she combines the tomatoes and rice.

Place the onion, garlic and courgette in a sauté pan, add 1 tablespoon of the tomato purée and season well with salt and pepper. Add 2–3 tablespoons of the EVOO, then stir and cook for 8–10 minutes over a medium–high heat, until the onion is soft and the courgette is starting to caramelize.

Add the rice to the pan, stir well to coat in the oil, and cook for about 2 minutes. This will help to seal the rice so that it doesn't soften too much in the oven. Add the canned tomatoes and half the vegetable stock, and simmer over a low–medium heat for 10 minutes, stirring occasionally.

Add the pine nuts and the herbs, then remove from the heat.

Preheat the oven to 180°C (160°C fan/350°F/Gas mark 4).

Cut a thin slice off the top of each fresh tomato and set aside for later. Using a teaspoon, carefully scoop out the seeds and membrane, finely chop them and add to the rice. Set the hollow tomatoes aside.

Slice the top off each pepper and trim the stems if they are very long. Scoop out and discard the seeds and membranes. Set aside the hollow peppers and 'lids' for later. Peel and chop the potatoes into large wedges.

Add the potatoes, tomatoes and peppers to a baking dish in which they will fit very snugly. Packing them fairly tightly will stop the peppers and tomatoes from collapsing in the oven.

Stir the parsley into the rice, check the seasoning and add more salt and pepper if needed. Spoon the rice into the peppers and tomatoes so that it almost spills out of the top. Cover with the reserved lids.

TIP
This recipe calls for a tomato knife, or one with a serrated edge.

EVOO TO PAIR
Something with tomato notes, like Koroneiki or Hojiblanca.

Stir the remaining tablespoon of tomato purée into the remaining vegetable stock, and carefully pour this over the peppers, tomatoes and potatoes. Drizzle with EVOO, then tightly cover the dish with foil.

Bake for 1 hour, then remove the foil and cook for another 20 minutes, until the peppers and tomatoes are nicely charred and the stock has reduced into a sauce. Let the dish cool for 10 minutes before serving. (It tastes even better the next day.)

Paella Valenciana

'Everybody has different ways of preparing paella,' explains my dear friend Estefanía Sánchez-Gómez Rodríguez, whose family has a café in Valencia. 'Some people use stock, others just use water, some people add snails, others add rosemary, some don't… This is how my family does it, and I can assure you that the result is optimal!'

Serves 6

- **100g (3½oz) dried butter beans**
- **2 large plum tomatoes or 1 large beef tomato**
- **225g (8oz) runner beans**
- **½–1 teaspoon saffron threads**
- **2–3 tablespoons extra virgin olive oil, plus extra to serve**
- **4 small chicken thighs, or 8 if not using rabbit**
- **1 rabbit, jointed (optional)**
- **100g (3½oz) chicken livers**
- **2 garlic cloves, crushed**
- **2 artichoke hearts, quartered**
- **½–1 teaspoon sweet paprika**
- **1.5 litres (2½ pints) chicken stock**
- **550g (1lb 4oz) bomba paella rice**
- **salt and freshly ground black pepper**
- **lemon wedges, to serve**

Soak the dried beans in a large bowl of cold water overnight. The next day, drain the beans, place them in a saucepan and cover generously with water. Bring to the boil, reduce the heat to a simmer and cook for 40–60 minutes, or until just tender. Drain and set aside.

Coarsely grate the tomatoes onto a plate. Trim the runner beans and cut into 2.5cm (1in) lengths. Soak the saffron in 1 tablespoon hot water.

Pour the measured EVOO into the centre of a large paella pan or a wide shallow pan, tilting it so that the oil covers the whole surface. Place over a medium heat. When hot, add the chicken thighs and rabbit pieces (if using) and season with salt. Fry until browned, then add the chicken livers and brown these too.

Push the meat to the edges of the pan. Place the garlic in the middle and cook for 1 minute. Add the butter beans, runner beans and artichokes. Cook for 3–4 minutes, stirring carefully so that you don't get burned. Stir in the grated tomato, and cook for another 2 minutes.

Quickly stir in the paprika, making sure it doesn't burn. Add enough stock to cover the ingredients. Bring the stock to the boil, then add the saffron and its soaking liquid. Gradually stir the rice into the bubbling pan, then reduce the heat to a simmer and cook for about 15 minutes.

Taste the stock and add more salt if necessary. Cook for another 5 minutes. Once the rice is al dente, turn off the heat and cover the paella with a lid or a sheet of foil. Allow to rest for 5 minutes so that it finishes cooking and the rice absorbs any remaining liquid.

Set the pan on the dining table, add a final drizzle of olive oil and garnish with lemon wedges.

EVOO TO PAIR
Hojiblanca, with its tomato notes and balance of bitter and spicy flavours, is a delight here, but an early-harvest Arbequina or Picual will also shine.

Slow-Cooked Lamb
with Red Pepper Salsa

In Greece, it's traditional to break the fast for Lent on Easter Sunday by feasting on lamb. Not only is lamb a part of the feast that begins right after the midnight service, but the whole next day you will find people roasting whole lambs (often on a spit) all over the neighbourhood. This kitchen-friendly version comes to us from Helena Moursellas, a bestselling Australian-born cookbook author and chef. Together with her twin sister Vikki, Helena shares her love of Greek food with the world, blending culinary expertise with a deep appreciation of the family's Thessalonikian heritage to create delicious, accessible recipes. In this version, the lamb is marinated overnight in the magic of EVOO, then cooked for 4½ hours, making it tender enough to fall apart at the touch of a fork. It's paired with a zingy roast pepper salsa and topped with caperberries, which work beautifully with roast potatoes for a hearty dinner, or serve it with a rainbow of salad leaves for a lighter meal. The best thing about this dish, according to Helena? 'You can throw it into the oven and give yourself plenty of time to get ready for when your guests arrive.' Win-win!

Serves 6

- 100ml (3½fl oz) extra virgin olive oil
- 4 garlic cloves, crushed
- 1 tablespoon dried oregano
- finely grated zest and juice of 1 unwaxed lemon
- 15g (½oz) oregano, leaves roughly chopped
- 1.8kg (4lb) bone-in lamb shoulder
- 250ml (9fl oz) vegetable stock or water
- 150g (5½oz) caperberries
- sea salt flakes and freshly ground black pepper

EVOO TO PAIR
Halkidiki, Koroneiki, Hojiblanca, Nocellara del Belice.

Place the EVOO in a bowl with the garlic, dried oregano, lemon zest and juice and half of the fresh oregano. Whisk together, then whisk in 1 tablespoon sea salt flakes and a generous twist of black pepper.

Sit the lamb in a roasting tray and stab holes in it using the point of a sharp knife. Pour over the garlicky marinade and use your hands to massage it into the meat on all sides. Cover and leave to marinate in the fridge overnight.

The following day, remove the lamb from the fridge an hour before you want to start cooking to bring it to room temperature.

Preheat the oven to 160°C (140°C fan/325°F/Gas mark 3).

Sprinkle the lamb with the remaining fresh oregano leaves, season again and pour the stock into the tray. Cover the joint with a large piece of nonstick baking paper, then tightly cover the tray with foil. Roast for 2½ hours.

FOR THE RED PEPPER SALSA

- 3 red peppers
- 4 tablespoons extra virgin olive oil
- 2 tablespoons finely chopped dill
- 2 tablespoons finely chopped parsley
- 1 teaspoon red wine vinegar

Remove the baking paper and foil and increase the oven temperature to 170°C/150°C fan/340°F/Gas mark 3½. Cook the lamb for a further 2 hours, basting with the tray juices every 15 minutes, until the lamb is tender and starting to fall off the bone. Add more stock or water to the tray if the lamb is drying out.

One hour before the lamb cooking time is up, start preparing the salsa. Place the peppers on a baking tray lined with nonstick baking paper, drizzle with 2 tablespoons of the EVOO and roast for 50–55 minutes, or until the skins have blistered and blackened. (The peppers could also be cooked under a hot grill or over a gas flame.)

Place the roasted peppers in a bowl, cover tightly with plastic wrap and leave to sit for 20 minutes, as the steam will help to loosen the skin.

Peel the blackened peppers, remove the seeds, then finely chop the flesh. Place in a bowl with the dill and parsley, the remaining 2 tablespoons EVOO and the vinegar. Season with sea salt flakes and freshly ground black pepper.

Remove the cooked lamb from the oven, cover loosely with foil and set aside to rest for 20 minutes. Then, using 2 forks, shred the meat from the bone and pile it onto a serving platter. Drizzle with the roasted pepper salsa, sprinkle with the caperberries and serve with your preferred accompaniments.

Pasta Anellini al Forno
with Fried Aubergines

'A little aperitivo?' Vania Sarullo says, as she welcomes us to the family mill in the Agrigento region of Sicily. We laugh, since what's in front of us is a massive plate of baked pasta, presented like a cake, on a table covered with other treats, all prepared by her mother. It is one of those show-stopping, homemade dishes that you'll find at a family Sunday lunch in Sicily. It instantly takes me back to my own youth, which featured a lot of baked ziti (large macaroni), because it was easy, hearty and wholesome, and you could feed the masses with one big dish. This is Sicilian nonna (granny) food, and it's about as comforting as it gets. In Sicily, this recipe is often baked in a large bundt tin lined with fried aubergine slices, with the saucy pasta packed into the middle. Once baked, the whole thing is turned out of the tin before serving in slices, like a cake. This is a simplified version, but no less delicious.

Serves 6

- **4 aubergines**
- **extra virgin olive oil, for frying, brushing and drizzling**
- **500g (1lb 2oz) anelletti pasta (little hoops, or another small shape)**
- **150g (5½oz) peas, fresh or frozen**
- **150g (5½oz) provolone, caciocavallo or Cheddar cheese, cubed**
- **100g (3½oz) Parmesan cheese, grated**
- **2 eggs, lightly beaten**
- **3 tablespoons fresh breadcrumbs**

Start by making the ragù. In a wide pan, heat 2 tablespoons of the EVOO over a low–medium heat and gently cook the onion, carrot and celery until soft. (This is your soffritto, a classic vegetable base for sauces.) Add the garlic and cook for another minute.

Add the minced beef to the pan, increase the heat to medium and fry for about 10 minutes, until brown all over. Pour in the wine, bring to the boil, then allow it to bubble gently until reduced by half.

Stir in the tomato purée, then the passata and season well with salt and pepper. Bring the ragù to the boil, reduce to a simmer and cook for about 45 minutes, until thickened, rich and glossy.

Meanwhile, trim the tops off the aubergines and cut the remainder into lengthways slices 5mm (¼in) thick. Heat 2 tablespoons EVOO in a large frying pan over a medium heat. When hot, fry the aubergine slices in batches until golden, adding more oil to the pan as needed.

While the aubergine is cooking, bring a large pan of salted water to the boil, add the pasta and cook until just al dente (so

FOR THE RAGÙ

- 4–6 tablespoons extra virgin olive oil
- 1 small onion, finely chopped
- 1 carrot, finely chopped
- 1 celery stick, trimmed and finely chopped
- 2 garlic cloves, crushed
- 500g (1lb 2oz) minced beef
- 200ml (7fl oz) red wine
- 2 tablespoons tomato purée
- 500ml (18fl oz) tomato passata
- salt and freshly ground black pepper

MAKE IT YOUR OWN
Courgette strips can be used instead of aubergine, and you can add more vegetables, such as chopped carrots, mushrooms or spinach, to the ragù. Using minced pork, venison or a mixture of pork and beef works well here too.

EVOO TO PAIR
The Sarullo family, who shared this recipe with us, like to use their delicate Biancolilla oil, but a sharper Tonda Iblea or Nocellara would also do well here.

slightly less time than the packet says). Drain and allow the pasta to cool slightly.

Preheat the oven to 190°C (170°C fan/375°F/Gas mark 5).

Tip the cooked pasta and ragù into a large bowl, add the peas, cubed cheese, grated Parmesan and eggs. Mix well to combine.

Brush a 40 x 20cm (16 x 9in) baking tin with EVOO and line the base and sides with the aubergine slices. Spoon in the pasta mixture, pressing it down firmly. Sprinkle with the breadcrumbs, drizzle with EVOO and bake for 30–35 minutes, until golden and crisp on top.

This is best served warm, so set aside in the tin to cool for a few minutes, then slice or scoop to serve.

Barbecue Lamb Chops & Charred Veg

with Olive Oil Marinade

South Africa, with its special climate, makes some of the best New World olive oil. Brenda and Nick Wilkinson didn't set out to become olive farmers and millers, but after being prescribed EVOO by a doctor and looking for a place to 'retire', they ended up with an olive grove in the Western Cape. At Rio Largo, they now look after thousands of trees – all of them Italian varieties originally planted by the Portuguese. I asked Brenda to share a recipe that reflects this unique region, and she came back with the idea for a braii, or South African barbecue. High-quality EVOO is perfect for marinating, since it's a great tenderizer, carries flavour and keeps the meat from drying out.

Serves 4

- 5 tablespoons extra virgin olive oil, plus extra to serve
- 2 garlic cloves, crushed
- 1 tablespoon chopped rosemary
- 2 unwaxed lemons
- 8 lamb loin chops
- 2 sweet red peppers
- 2 baby courgettes
- 1 red onion
- 1 small butternut squash
- leaves from 2 sprigs of thyme
- sea salt flakes and freshly ground black pepper
- crusty bread, to serve

TIP
Given the recipe's origins, Brenda advises: 'Remember to serve with some fabulous South African wine!'

EVOO TO PAIR
Varieties like Frantoio, Leccino, Moraiolo and Coratina work nicely.

Place 3 tablespoons of the EVOO in a large bowl, add the garlic, rosemary and finely grated zest from 1 lemon. Mix well, then add the lamb chops, season with salt and pepper and massage the marinade into the meat. Cover and place in the fridge for 1–2 hours.

Preheat the barbecue until the coals are hot and glowing.

Quarter and deseed the peppers, halve the courgettes lengthways, and cut the onion into wedges. Slice the unpeeled squash into rounds about 1cm (½in) thick. Toss these veggies in a bowl containing the remaining 2 tablespoons EVOO, the thyme and some sea salt flakes and black pepper.

Cook the vegetables in a cast-iron pan on the barbecue, or directly on the rack over the hot coals, until they are charred and tender.

Place the chops over medium–hot coals and barbecue for 3–4 minutes per side, depending on thickness, until golden outside and just pink inside.

Serve the chops and veggies with lemon wedges for squeezing over, and offer crusty bread alongside.

Pljukanci
with Rocket & Prosciutto

This recipe comes to us from the gastronomical wonder that is the Istrian peninsula in Croatia, and our award-winning producer, Lena, whose family makes small-batch EVOOs from rare varieties of olives found in the region. Pljukanci is a typical Istrian pasta eaten with all manner of sauces. 'Prosciutto and rocket sauce is the most popular,' says Lena. 'Sometimes, my mum, my aunt and me sit at the table and make pljukanci while chatting about this and that. Kids are often involved, as it's fun!'

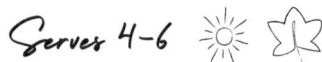 Serves 4–6

- 200g (7oz) '00' flour, plus extra for dusting
- 200g (7oz) plain flour
- 2 big pinches of salt
- 250ml (9fl oz) freshly boiled water
- 2 tablespoons extra virgin olive oil

FOR THE SAUCE
- 2–3 tablespoons extra virgin olive oil
- 2 garlic cloves, thinly sliced
- 100g (3½oz) prosciutto, sliced into ribbons
- good splash of white wine
- 200g (7oz) cherry tomatoes, halved
- good handful of rocket
- salt and freshly ground black pepper
- freshly shaved Parmesan cheese, to serve

EVOO TO PAIR
Leccino, Buža, Taggiasca.

Sift both flours and the salt into a large bowl. Mixing continuously with a wooden spoon or spatula, gradually add the hot water and olive oil. Once all added, knead the dough until it comes together in a ball. Turn the dough onto a clean floured work surface and knead for about 5 minutes, until smooth and soft. Cover the dough with the upturned bowl and leave to rest for 15 minutes.

To make pljukanci, pinch an olive-sized piece of dough and roll it between your hands or on the work surface until it is about 5cm (2in) long and thicker in the middle than at the ends. Place on a lightly floured tray and continue until all the dough has been used up. Cover with a clean tea towel.

Bring a large pan of salted water to the boil. Add the pljukanci and cook for 5 minutes, until they are tender and float to the surface.

Meanwhile, prepare the sauce. Pour the EVOO into a large frying pan, add the garlic and cook over a medium heat for 1 minute to soften. Add the prosciutto and fry until crisp, stirring often. Pour in the wine, then add the tomatoes and cook for another minute to soften them.

Using a slotted spoon, transfer the pljukanci to the frying pan and add 1–2 ladlefuls of the pasta water. Toss to combine, adding a little more pasta water if needed to make a light sauce. Add the rocket, season with salt and pepper, and stir until wilted. Serve immediately with Parmesan, more pepper and a generous drizzle of EVOO.

Tassos's Aubergine Bake

Here's the sort of recipe that can evolve as you go with whatever you have on hand. The original base came to me from Tassos Kyriakides, a professor at the Yale School of Public Health and co-founder of the Yale Olive Sciences and Health Institute. He's also a certified olive oil sommelier. While Tassos keeps this bake vegan and more akin to a pasta sauce, I've shaped it with flavours from the eastern Mediterranean, closer to Tassos's place of origin in Cyprus. However you make it, though, the result is flavourful, hearty and healthy.

Serves 4–6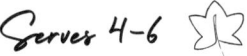

- 3 aubergines, cut into large bite-sized pieces
- 2 red onions, cut into wedges or thick slices
- 4 garlic cloves, sliced
- 2 teaspoons za'atar
- 100ml (3½fl oz) extra virgin olive oil, plus extra to serve
- 400g (14oz) can chopped tomatoes
- 400g (14oz) can or jar chickpeas, drained and rinsed
- 1 teaspoon Aleppo pepper (optional)
- 1–2 tablespoons pomegranate molasses
- 3 tablespoons chopped flat leaf parsley
- 200g (7oz) Greek yoghurt
- salt and freshly ground black pepper

Preheat the oven to 200°C (180°C fan/400°F/Gas mark 6).

Place the aubergines and onions in a large baking tray and sprinkle with the garlic and za'atar. Drizzle over the EVOO, season with salt and pepper, and mix with your hands to coat the vegetables in the oil and spices.

Bake for 25–30 minutes, until the aubergine slices are soft and starting to caramelize at the edges.

Add the tomatoes, chickpeas and pul biber (if using) and stir to combine. Return to the oven for a further 15 minutes, until the vegetables are soft and everything has cooked into a delicious saucy medley.

Serve warm, drizzled with more EVOO and some pomegranate molasses, then sprinkled with parsley and a dollop of yogurt.

MAKE IT YOUR OWN
Add sliced courgette or sweet peppers, or a handful of fresh cherry tomatoes, depending on the season. Crumble over some feta to make it creamy, and try swapping the chickpeas for butter beans or lentils. Add a handful of chopped dill and pomegranate seeds. Alternatively, sprinkle with toasted pine nuts or add a handful of olives. A drizzle of tahini just before serving is also great.

TIP
While this dish can be served on its own, it's also delicious over pasta, sweet potatoes or couscous.

EVOO TO PAIR
A bold Hojiblanca from Spain, a Coratina from Italy, or a Lebanese Souri or Greek Koroneiki will match the za'atar's brightness.

Focaccia

Pillowy, delicious and perfect for mopping up every last drop of olive oil, you can't go wrong with a good focaccia. This recipe uses a mixture of plain flour and bread flour for a slightly lighter dough. The stretch and fold method is not only more fun than traditional kneading, but it also allows for a higher hydration dough, which makes a loaf with lots of lovely air bubbles. I like a simple salt and rosemary topping, but you could add sun-dried tomatoes, olives, sliced preserved lemons or anything else that takes your fancy. This tried-and-tested version comes courtesy of our team baker and resident marathon runner, Imogen Dickinson, an expert on carbs and good fats.

Serves 8

- 300–340ml (10–11½fl oz) lukewarm water
- 7–8 tablespoons extra virgin olive oil
- 7g (¼oz) sachet fast-action dried yeast
- 1 teaspoon honey, agave or golden syrup
- 250g (9oz) strong white flour
- 250g (9oz) plain flour
- 6g (about 1 teaspoon) table salt
- sea salt flakes, to taste
- leaves from 3 sprigs of rosemary

Pour 325ml (11fl oz) of the lukewarm water into a bowl or jug, add 1 tablespoon of the EVOO, then the yeast and honey and mix to combine.

Place the flours and measured salt in a large bowl and mix together. Pour in the yeast mixture and mix by hand until a dough starts to form. It might look a bit rough, but don't worry – the liquid doesn't need to be fully mixed in, and the dough should be on the wet side, so if it looks too dry, add more water a teaspoon at a time.

Cover the bowl and leave to rest at room temperature for 30 minutes. This allows the flour to hydrate (fully absorb the water) and the gluten proteins to begin developing, leading to a more aromatic, flavourful and easier-to-handle dough.

After 30 minutes, dampen your hands slightly and perform the first set of stretches and folds. This involves gently lifting up the dough from one side of the bowl, stretching it upwards, then folding it back down on itself. Give the bowl a quarter turn and repeat the stretching and folding a further 3–4 times, with a quarter turn after each fold. Cover the dough and leave to rest at room temperature for 30 minutes.

Repeat the above step another 3 times, resting the dough for 30 minutes in between each set of stretches and folds.

After the final stretch and fold, cover the bowl and leave the dough to rise for 2 hours at room temperature. (You can also do this part overnight in the fridge – the yeast action is slower, but the dough will still rise.)

When the rising time is nearly up, pour 1–2 tablespoons EVOO into a 23 x 33cm (9 x 13in) baking tray and swirl it around to cover the base. Carefully transfer the dough to the tray, then lift up each side of it in turn and fold it into the middle, forming a rectangle shape. This will be a bit messy and slippery as the dough will be oily.

Flip the dough over so that it's seam-side down and drizzle with 2 tablespoons EVOO. Cover loosely with plastic wrap and leave to rise again at room temperature for 45–60 minutes, until the dough is puffy and bubbles are appearing on top.

Preheat the oven to 220°C (200°C fan/425°F/Gas mark 7).

Press your fingertips (or the end of a wooden spoon if you have long nails) into the dough to create lots of nice dimples.

Place 2 tablespoons EVOO in a bowl and mix with the remaining tablespoon water. Pour this mixture over the dimpled dough – the water creates a little more steam in the oven, which gives a nice crust and the oil gives the focaccia its characteristic flavour and golden colour.

Sprinkle 2–3 teaspoons flaky salt and the rosemary leaves over the top. If you have the time or inclination, you can press the herb sprigs into the dough instead.

Bake the focaccia for 20–25 minutes, or until well risen and golden brown. Remove from the oven and, while still warm, drizzle with the final tablespoon (or more!) of EVOO.

Now for the hardest part: wait 20–30 minutes for the bread to cool before tucking in.

TIP
I like to use one EVOO for the mix, and a different one to finish. Usually more delicate and buttery in the blend and then one with more vibrant, herby notes to drizzle and dip.

EVOO TO PAIR
Go for a medium intensity, with buttery notes in the mix.

Desserts & Finishers

'We want people to know the toil behind making a good olive oil. It is not simply a one- or two-day harvest and milling. It is a constant battle to get to that point. But still we refuse to give up and settle for less than the best quality. That moment in the mill when we see our first olive oil drizzling out and taste it at last – it makes every day in the groves worth the while.'

—Maria Amargiotaki, producer, Heraklion, Crete

Sweet Buns

Escarpiada

With this recipe, Marije and Gui Passos, producers of Passeite olive oils in Portugal, are sharing more of the sweeter side of EVOO. Escarpiada means 'steep', and the unique shape of these layered buns, flavoured with soft brown sugar, cinnamon and olive oil, brings to mind Portugal's hilly landscape. The oldest known recipe for escarpiada dates back more than a hundred years and was for a large loaf baked in a clay pot, but these days individual portions are more popular. Traditionally associated with festive periods, such as Easter, these delicious buns are now sold throughout the year in bakeries across the country. Recipes for escarpiada can vary from region to region, with Marije's coming from her municipality of Condeixa-a-Nova in central Portugal. It features on the recipe cards given out as part of the olive oil tasting classes Marije and Gui hold at their groves outside Coimbra, as their beautiful Galega variety works really well in this kind of bake.

Makes 8–10

- 250g (9oz) strong white flour
- 250g (9oz) plain flour, plus extra for dusting
- ¾ sachet (5g) fast-action dried yeast
- ½ teaspoon salt
- 350ml (12fl oz) lukewarm water

FOR THE SUGAR MIX
- 150–200g (5½–7oz) light brown soft sugar
- 1 tablespoon ground cinnamon
- 8 tablespoons extra virgin olive oil

Place both flours in the bowl of a stand mixer fitted with a dough hook, then stir in the yeast and salt. With the mixer running at a slow speed, add the warm water and mix to combine. Scrape down the sides of the bowl, then continue working the dough at a medium speed for about 8 minutes, until smooth and elastic. Cover the bowl and set aside to rise at room temperature for about 45 minutes, or until the dough has nearly doubled in size.

Meanwhile, mix the sugar and cinnamon together in a bowl. Line a baking tray with nonstick baking paper.

Turn the risen dough onto a lightly floured work surface. Divide into equal pieces of 50–60g (1¾–2¼oz) and rolls into balls.

Working on one ball at a time, use your hands and a rolling pin to shape the dough into a rectangle measuring about 12 x 18cm (5 x 7in). Brush the top with EVOO and sprinkle generously with the sugar mixture. Fold the dough in half like a book to encase the sugar. Brush the top with more oil and sprinkle with more sugar, then fold the dough into thirds, like a letter, starting at one of the short sides. Place the bun on the

prepared tray, seam-side down. Repeat this process with the remaining dough balls, spacing them well apart on the tray to allow for rising.

Brush the top of the buns with EVOO and sprinkle with more sugar mix – don't be shy! Cover loosely and leave to rest and rise for about 40 minutes at room temperature.

Preheat the oven to 190°C (170°C fan/375°F/Gas mark 5), then bake the buns for 12–15 minutes, until golden, crisp and light. When the baking time is almost up, turn the buns over and return to the oven for another minute to bake the base.

When ready, turn the buns right side up again and brush the tops with a little of the syrup in the tray. Set aside to cool to room temperature before serving.

EVOO TO PAIR
Delicate and buttery styles like Galega, Arbequina, Manaki and Ogliarola.

Roasted Pineapple
with Pink Peppercorns & Coconut Ice Cream

When I did my sommelier training and first started to hear from other sommeliers about interesting pairings with olive oil, pineapple kept coming up. Much like chocolate, it's a flavour you can lean into with a delicate, fruity EVOO, or you can push the boundaries with a contrasting oil to show true complexity. When Marcelo Scofano, the Brazilian olive oil judge and sensory analyst, shared a sweet recipe that represents how his country takes EVOO to the next level, I knew it had to have a place in this book. A simple fruity treat to serve with ice creams, cakes and creams.

Serves 6

- 1 large ripe pineapple
- 2 tablespoons light, brown soft sugar
- 1–2 teaspoons pink peppercorns, lightly crushed
- finely grated zest and juice of 1 unwaxed lime
- 4 tablespoons ripe or medium-intensity extra virgin olive oil (see suggestions below), plus extra to serve
- pinch of sea salt flakes
- coconut ice cream, to serve

Preheat the oven to 200°C (180°C fan/400°F/Gas mark 6).

Slice the top and bottom off the pineapple and stand it upright on the chopping board. Starting at the top and working down, slice off the skin in strips. Use the point of the knife to remove the 'eyes'.

Cut the pineapple in half vertically, then cut each half in half again, so you have 4 long wedges. Cut the tough central core out of each wedge, then cut each wedge into diagonal slices 2cm (¾in) thick .

Place the pineapple in a roasting tray, add the brown sugar, peppercorns, lime zest and juice and 2 tablespoons of the EVOO. Mix to coat well, then roast for about 25 minutes, until golden and caramelized.

Arrange the pineapple on a plate with the roasting juices, sprinkle with sea salt flakes and drizzle with the remaining 2 tablespoons EVOO.

Serve immediately with scoops of coconut ice cream, finishing with a little more EVOO.

MAKE IT YOUR OWN
You could use crushed dried chilli flakes in place of the pink peppercorns. Other flavours, such as star anise and vanilla, are also good with pineapple.
Try adding a splash of rum to the pineapple before roasting.

EVOO TO PAIR
A fruity oil like an early harvest Picual, Hojiblanca or Arbequina.

Lemon & EVOO Cake

Everyone needs a simple sponge cake recipe, and this one comes from Marina Segura Gómez of Peña Luna near Málaga, our youngest producer. She's also one who's pushing the boat out when it comes to flavour and experimenting with aromatic oils. This cake, inspired by her lemon olive oil, can be paired with the roasted pinneapple on the previous page or the olive oil chantilly opposite.

Serves 8–10

- 5 eggs
- 200g (7oz) extra virgin olive oil, plus extra for drizzling
- 250g (9oz) caster sugar
- finely grated zest of 2 unwaxed lemons
- 250g (9oz) plain or '00' flour
- 2 teaspoons baking powder
- pinch of salt
- icing sugar, to dust

Preheat the oven to 180°C (160°C fan/350°F/Gas mark 4). Grease the base and sides of a deep, 23cm (9in) cake tin, then line with nonstick baking paper.

Place the eggs and EVOO in a large mixing bowl and beat with an electric whisk for 2–3 minutes, until pale and light.

Add the caster sugar and beat again for a minute or so, until well aerated. Add the lemon zest and mix again.

Sift the flour, baking powder and salt into the egg mixture and beat again, until smooth and thoroughly combined.

Spoon the batter into the prepared tin and spread evenly. Bake for about 45 minutes, until the cake is well risen and golden, and a skewer inserted in the middle comes out clean. Set the cake aside to cool in the tin.

Transfer the cake to a serving plate, dust with icing sugar and serve in slices with a drizzle of EVOO.

MAKE IT YOUR OWN
To make a simple lemon glaze to spoon over the cake as it cools in the tin, add 2–3 tablespoons icing sugar to the juice of 2 lemons and mix well.
The cake can also be made with almond flour and polenta to make it gluten-free.

TIP
Start with a lemon-infused or aromatic olive oil instead of regular EVOO, and it'll be quite a treat!

EVOO TO PAIR
A later harvest, more delicate oil like Arbequina, Manaki or Biancolilla.

Olive Oil Chantilly

'I learned about this idea from André Cabrita, a Portuguese chef who loves our Galega variety,' explains Ana Cardoso of Tratturo de Fronteira groves in Alentejo, Portugal. This simple sweetened emulsion can be used to accompany fruit or a simple sponge cake – drizzled with olive oil, of course. This is one of many simple swaps you can make to use more extra virgin olive oil in baking recipes, rather than just dairy fats. Making this with different EVOOs will show you how this one ingredient can transform the flavour profile of the chantilly.

Serves 8

- 500ml (18fl oz) double cream
- 1–2 tablespoons icing sugar
- 3–4 tablespoons extra virgin olive oil

Start by chilling a mixing bowl in the freezer for 30 minutes before use, as this will help the cream to whip up faster.

Pour the cream into the cold bowl, add 1 tablespoon icing sugar and begin whisking with a hand-held electric whisk at a medium speed.

Once the cream reaches soft peaks, turn the speed to low and very slowly drizzle in the olive oil as you whisk. You want the oil to fold in without splitting the cream. The moment the cream looks glossy and just holds its shape – stop. Overdo it and you'll end up in butter territory.

Chill until ready to serve with the dessert or cake of your choice.

MAKE IT YOUR OWN
Serve this cream with sliced mangoes and fresh mint for a delicious dessert, or try it pavlova-style with meringue and berries.
Add a tablespoon of matcha powder for covering simple cakes.

TIP
As with conventional Chantilly, if you refrigerate this after mixing, you'll most likely need to whisk it again briefly before use.
Ana's tip: 'If you're after a subtly sweet chantilly, add just one tablespoon of icing sugar, but for a more dessert-forward version, go for two.'

EVOO TO PAIR
A fruity oil, such as Galega, Arbequina, Taggiasca or Biancolilla, is ideal.

Olive Oil Biscuits

with Lemon & Thyme

A simple crowd-pleaser of a cookie, more interesting than your standard shortbread – the lemon and thyme give a little Mediterranean feel to an English tea biscuit. This is another recipe from our team baker, Imogen Dickinson, who wanted to make a treat showcasing olive oil that every member of the team could eat, from the vegans to the gluten-free. You can also make them into an extra-indulgent sandwich biscuit, as shown here, using vegan cream cheese icing, buttercream or sweetened mascarpone.

Makes 18–20

- 180g (6¼oz) plain flour (if using GF flour, add 20–40g/¾–1½oz extra)
- 40g (1½oz) caster sugar
- 20g (¾oz) icing sugar
- finely grated zest of ½ unwaxed lemon
- leaves from 2–3 sprigs of thyme
- ¼ teaspoon vanilla extract
- 75g (2¾oz) butter or non-dairy alternative, diced
- 2 tablespoons extra virgin olive oil

Place the flour, sugars, lemon zest, thyme and vanilla extract in a mixing bowl. Add the butter and rub in with your fingers until the mixture resembles breadcrumbs. Use a wooden spoon to mix in the olive oil and form a dough. If the mixture seems a bit dry, add a little more oil.

Sit the dough on a sheet of baking paper on the work surface and form into a ball. Flatten into a disc and use a rolling pin to roll out to a thickness of 3mm (⅛in). Slide the paper and dough onto a baking sheet and chill for 30 minutes to firm up.

Preheat the oven to 180°C (160°C fan/350°F/Gas mark 4). Line a baking sheet with nonstick baking paper.

Using a 5cm (2in) round cutter, stamp 18–20 circles out of the chilled dough, then transfer to the prepared sheet. Gather any dough offcuts into a ball, re-roll and stamp out more circles.

Bake for about 15 minutes, until firm and starting to turn golden at the edges.

MAKE IT YOUR OWN
Replace the lemon zest with another citrus flavour, such as orange or lime. Some finely chopped nuts, especially almonds, would be a good addition.

EVOO TO PAIR
Lighter, fruitier varieties, such as Arbequina and Biancolilla, work well here, but anything fruity can be nice.

Carolina's Chocorocas

The beauty of an EVOO variety such as Arbequina is that its delicate fruitiness and almond-like notes make it perfect for baking and desserts. This recipe for truffles comes to us from Carolina Domínguez of Pago Peñarrubia, whose family groves are in Albacete, Spain. As her main variety is Arbequina, she wanted to share a recipe using EVOO instead of butter. 'The chocolate melts better in the mouth and doesn't leave that heavy feeling on the tongue that butter does,' she explains. And like all high-quality EVOO, it's a carrier of flavour and elevates notes from the chocolate that regular oils and butter might drown out.

Makes about 40

- 400g (14oz) good-quality plain dark chocolate (80% cocoa solids)
- 175ml (6fl oz) extra virgin olive oil
- good pinch of sea salt flakes
- 50g (1¾oz) unsweetened cocoa powder

Break the chocolate into squares and melt in a heatproof bowl over a pan of barely simmering water, or in the microwave on a low setting. Stir until smooth, making sure the temperature doesn't exceed 50°C (122°F), then remove from the heat. Add the olive oil and stir with a spatula until the mixture is thoroughly emulsified.

Pour into a 30 x 20cm (12 x 8in) tray lined with nonstick baking paper and refrigerate for 24 hours, until set firm.

Once firm, sprinkle the chocolate slab with sea salt flakes. Warm a long-bladed knife in a jug of hot water, dry the blade, then cut the slab into bite-sized pieces.

Tip the cocoa powder into another tray and roll each truffle in it to coat. Dust the bottom of a large, airtight container with cocoa and place the truffles in it, ensuring the pieces don't touch each other. Store in the coldest part of the fridge.

MAKE IT YOUR OWN
Make it extra with a topping of your own: spinkle crushed peppercorns, pistachios, or even drizzle some tahini over the top.

TIP
It's important to store the truffles in the fridge and take them out just before eating.

EVOO TO PAIR
Arbequina, or a delicate style, such as Manaki, or riper flavour, such as Galega.

Greek Christmas Cookies
with Honey & Orange

The twelfth day of Christmas – 6 January, aka Epiphany – marks the end of the traditional Christmas season, with treats being enjoyed all across the Mediterranean. Should you find yourself in Greece around this time of year, you'll likely have a melomakarona, or 'honey cookie'. Every year, our producer Maria and her family in Crete share photos of themselves making them in the lead-up to the end of the Christmas festivities. Lifted by the notes of winter citrus, these biscuits are full of those festive flavours that make your house smell amazing!

Makes 25–30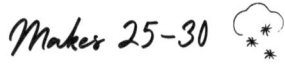

- 140ml (4½fl oz) freshly squeezed orange juice
- 1 teaspoon bicarbonate of soda
- 3 tablespoons clear honey
- 25ml (¾fl oz) brandy
- 500g (1lb 2oz) plain flour
- 160g (5¾oz) fine semolina
- 1 teaspoon ground cinnamon
- 150g (5½oz) caster sugar
- 220ml (7½fl oz) extra virgin olive oil
- finely grated zest of ½ orange

FOR THE SYRUP
- 200g (7oz) caster sugar
- 140ml (4½fl oz) water
- 2 cinnamon sticks
- 3 strips of orange peel
- 2 whole cloves
- 60g (2¼oz) clear honey

FOR THE TOPPING
- 50g (1¾oz) very finely chopped nuts (such as walnuts and sesame seeds)
- ground cinnamon, to taste

Start by making the syrup. Combine the sugar, water, cinnamon sticks, orange peel and cloves in a small saucepan. Bring to the boil over a low–medium heat to dissolve the sugar. Simmer for 3–4 minutes, until thickened slightly. Remove from the heat, add the honey and leave to cool.

Preheat the oven to 160°C (140°C fan/325°F/Gas mark 3) and line 2 baking sheets with nonstick baking paper.

To make the biscuits, place the orange juice and bicarbonate of soda in a small bowl and mix until foaming. Add the honey and brandy and mix to combine.

In another bowl, mix the flour, semolina, cinnamon and caster sugar. Add the olive oil, orange zest and orange juice mixture. Mix until thoroughly combined.

Using your hands, shape the dough into walnut-sized balls (about 40g/1½oz each), but do not overwork the mixture or the cookies will be hard and tough, and will not absorb the syrup. Slightly flatten the balls into oval shapes and arrange on the lined baking sheets, spacing them well apart.

Using a fork, prick the top of each cookie 2 or 3 times. Bake for about 18 minutes, until golden brown.

Using a slotted spoon, dip each hot biscuit in the cold syrup for 30 seconds – not too long as you don't want them to fall apart or become soggy. Allow the excess syrup to drip off, then transfer to a tray.

EVOO TO PAIR
A late-harvest Koroneiki is commonly used, but also Tsounati, Kalamon or Athinolia. Arbequina would also work well.

Top with chopped nuts and a pinch of cinnamon, gently pushing the nuts into the cookies so they stick.

These cookies will keep well for about 4 days (or even a week or more!) stored in an airtight container.

EVOO & Citrus Granita

One of those simple treats that just brightens up a meal. Granita goes back to ancient Mesopotamia and has been a tradition in Sicily since the island was under Arab rule in the 9th century – with the Sicillians putting their own local spin on it. Light, refreshing and easy to make, this particular version comes to us from Phoebe Liebling, a registered nutritional therapist who's all about easy, accessible ways to have a fuller, healthier life.We love her recipes and her ingredient tips for better overall well-being. You can make this a completely whole-food dessert by using honey instead of sugar.

Serves 2

- 200ml (7fl oz) freshly squeezed orange juice, plus the finely grated zest of 1 orange
- 100ml (3½fl oz) freshly squeezed lemon juice
- 2 tablespoons extra virgin olive oil, plus extra to serve
- 1–2 tablespoons sugar or raw honey, to taste
- pinch of sea salt

Whisk all the ingredients together in a bowl, then pour into a shallow container and freeze for 45–60 minutes.

Using a fork, scrape the ice crystals forming around the edges of the mixture to break them up and combine them with the unfrozen middle. Return the mixture to the freezer for another 30–45 minutes, then fork again to break up the ice crystals. Repeat this once more after another 45 minutes in the freezer.

After a total of 3–4 hours, you should be left with a beautifully smooth granita.

Serve in chilled glasses with a final drizzle of olive oil on top.

MAKE IT YOUR OWN
Phoebe recommends pairing this granita with strained yogurt, fresh figs or pomegranate seeds and walnuts. It's also lovely with some basil and mint leaves.

EVOO TO PAIR
Early harvest delicate varieties like Biancolilla, Leccino or Arbequina.

Mini Chocolate Cupcakes
with Chilli & EVOO

'This is a very simple and flavourful dessert that really enhances olive oil as an ingredient,' says Lena, our producer in Istria, Croatia. 'I tried it first years ago in one of my favourite local restaurants, the Batelina, owned by the chef David Skoko (he crossed swords with chef Ramsay in the TV series *Gordon Ramsay: Uncharted*). By chance, I became really good friends with David's wife Ana, a chef herself, who was more than happy to give me the recipe for these little 'perline', as they call them.'

Makes 20–24

- 400g (14oz) plain dark chocolate (60–70% cocoa solids)
- 110ml (3¾fl oz) extra virgin olive oil, plus extra to serve
- 100g (3½oz) caster sugar
- 3–5g (½–1 teaspoon) chilli powder
- pinch of sea salt flakes, plus extra to serve (optional)
- 2 large eggs, lightly beaten
- 80g (2¾oz) '00' flour
- 20g (¾oz) unsweetened cocoa powder
- vanilla ice cream, to serve

Break the chocolate in small chunks, place in a heatproof bowl, then add the EVOO, caster sugar, chilli powder and salt. Set the bowl over a pan of barely simmering water and melt the chocolate and oil together, stirring until smooth. Remove from the heat and allow to cool for 10 minutes.

Preheat the oven to 180°C (160°C fan/350°F/Gas mark 4). Line 2 x 12-hole bun trays with paper cases.

Stir the eggs into the chocolate until just combined. Sift in the flour and cocoa powder, then beat until smooth and thoroughly combined.

Spoon the mixture into the paper cases, filling them half full. Bake for about 10 minutes, until the cakes are set. Sprinkle with sea salt flakes, if you like.

Serve lukewarm or cold, drizzled with a peppery EVOO and a scoop of vanilla ice cream.

MAKE IT YOUR OWN
Pair with the olive oil chantilly on page 171, or add a berries to garnish.

EVOO TO PAIR
Buža from Istria would be really nice, but Leccino, Galega or Koroneiki would all work too.

Vegan Chocolate Mousse
with Olive Oil

The mighty chickpea has quite a range. Apart from the legume being used in all sorts of recipes, its liquid, aquafaba, has been used for some time now as a vegan replacement for egg whites in cocktails, such as whisky sour and gin fizz. Less known is how well it folds in with chocolate and sugar to make this super-easy vegan dessert. The extra virgin olive oil gives it a particularly creamy texture, while bringing a nutty vibrance to the chocolate itself.

Serves 2–4

- **100g (3½oz) plain dark chocolate (64–70% cocoa solids), broken into pieces**
- **50ml (2fl oz) aquafaba (chickpea water)**
- **20–25g (¾–1oz) caster sugar**
- **2 tablespoons extra virgin olive oil, plus extra to serve**
- **½ orange**
- **sea salt flakes**

Break the chocolate into squares and melt in a heatproof bowl set over a pan of barely simmering water, or in the microwave on a low setting. Stir until smooth, making sure the temperature doesn't exceed 50°C (122°F), then remove from the heat and leave to cool slightly for 3–4 minutes.

Whisk the aquafaba until it forms stiff peaks, then gradually whisk in the sugar a tablespoon at a time. Continue to whisk until the mixture is glossy and holds stiff peaks.

Add the olive oil to the melted chocolate and whisk gently to combine. Using a large spoon, fold in a tablespoonful of the aquafaba to loosen, then fold in the remainder, being careful not to knock out too much air.

Pour into small glasses or bowls, cover and chill for a couple of hours to set.

Just before serving, grate orange zest over the top of each mousse, drizzle with EVOO and sprinkle with sea salt. Garnish with a thin slice of the orange.

MAKE IT YOUR OWN
Add a splash of espresso or rum.
Introduce some heat with a pinch of chilli powder.
Serve topped with chopped nuts, such as pistachios.
Swap out the orange for another seasonal fruit, such as strawberries or rhubarb.

EVOO TO PAIR
Choose Biancollila, Manaki or Arbequina for something delicate.
Opt for an oil from Istria or Tuscany for a stronger flavour.

Mango & Olive Oil Sorbet

Like pineapple and olive oil (see page 169), mango and olive oil is one of those pairings many sommeliers go on about. Vibrant, bitterly sweet and fragrant fruit can showcase a high-quality EVOO in a new and interesting way. Likewise, a good oil will elevate the fruit, changing the whole experience. The Alphonso mango season is short, but these mangoes have a superior texture and flavour, so it's worth keeping an eye out for them – you can literally taste the sun. First tested by Marly Zemsta on our team, this recipe is now a go-to for us at events when the weather warms up. See overleaf for a photo.

Serves 4

- **2–3 ripe Alphonso or Honey mangoes**
- **75ml (2½fl oz) extra virgin olive oil, plus extra to serve**
- **juice of 1 lemon**
- **2–3 tablespoons caster sugar**
- **pinch of salt**

Peel the mangoes and slice the flesh away from the stone. Roughly chop the fruit and tip into a blender or food processor.

Add the EVOO, lemon juice, sugar and salt, then blend until smooth. Transfer to a lidded plastic container and freeze for about 3 hours, until the mixture is almost frozen solid.

Scoop the frozen mango mixture back into the blender or processor and whizz again until creamy. Return to the freezer for a couple of hours before serving in scoops with a drizzle of EVOO.

MAKE IT YOUR OWN
Add freshly torn mint on top.
For spice, it's lush with Tajín seasoning or chilli flakes on top.

EVOO TO PAIR
Early harvest Picual, Hojiblanca or a delicate Galega.

Olive Oil Ice Cream

Pairing ice cream with extra virgin olive oil might sound strange, but this is hands down the combination that has surprised and excited our community the most. The olive oil makes the ice cream somehow even more creamy, smooth and decadent, while also giving it a subtle savoury/sweet flavour, a little like that you get from salted caramel. It was the perfect serve to launch Citizens of Soil with, showing how olive oil could perform in an unexpected pairing. The method for incorporating EVOO into a homemade ice cream was shared with us by James Toth and Laura Petersen, former head chef and pastry chef respectively at Michelin-starred Cornerstone in London.

Serves 8

- **90g (3¼oz) egg yolks**
- **90g (3¼oz) caster sugar**
- **800ml (27fl oz) milk**
- **2 teaspoons vanilla extract or bean paste, or finely grated zest of ½ unwaxed lemon (optional)**
- **125ml (4fl oz) extra virgin olive oil**
- **5g (1 teaspoon) sea salt flakes, plus extra to serve**

Whisk the egg yolks and sugar together in a heatproof bowl until pale yellow and smooth.

Heat the milk in a saucepan until just below simmering, then pour into the egg mixture, whisking continuously until smooth and thoroughly combined. Add the vanilla or lemon zest (if using).

Pour the mixture back into the pan and cook over a low heat, stirring now and then until the custard coats the back of a spoon and reaches 82°C (180°F). Do not allow the custard to boil or the eggs will scramble and the mixture will be grainy.

Remove the pan from heat and pour in about half the olive oil in a slow, steady stream, whisking continuously to combine. Add the salt.

Strain the custard into a clean bowl, set aside to cool, then chill for at least 2 hours until completely cold.

The custard can now be churned in an ice-cream machine – this gives the best result. Alternatively, freeze in a lidded plastic container and stir once an hour for 5 hours with a hand whisk or electric mixer. Finally, freeze until firm.

Serve in scoops drizzled with the remaining EVOO and a sprinkle of sea salt flakes.

MAKE IT YOUR OWN
I like to serve this is in citrus halves. Slice an orange or lemon in half horizontally, scoop out the flesh, then freeze the hollow shells. Serve the ice cream in the shells. I like to grate citrus zest over the top, but you can also sprinkle cocoa nibs, sweetened leftover toasted breadcrumbs, or fresh herbs, such as mint or basil.

EVOO TO PAIR
Later-harvest, more delicate options suit most people best, so try Arbequina, Manaki, Galega or Leccino.

Index

Acknowledgements

ABOUT THE AUTHOR

Sarah Fulton Vachon is a leading olive oil expert and educator in the UK who's trained everyone from high-street chains to Michelin-starred restaurant teams. As the olive oil sommelier and founder behind Citizens of Soil, she curates a line-up of award-winning extra virgin olive oils for their monthly Olive Oil Club. She's a champion of women in farming, and partners with small-batch producers who practise regenerative agriculture. Sarah made the Telegraph and NatWest '100 Female Entrepreneurs to Watch' list and is a member of Women in Olive Oil, a global network that empowers education and advancement of women in the industry.

In closing: to *olive* the mad producers out there...

'Madness.' This is the word our producer in Tuscany, Fabrizio Lazi, used to describe the people who go into high-quality extra virgin olive oil. And he's not wrong. It's a path driven by passion. To be at the mercy of nature, and at the forefront of preparing for an unpredictable climate, is not for the faint of heart. These people are trying to make space for artisanship in a commodity category – a system that has been constructed for mass-production and high-process, not thriving nature and healthy communities. The juice – quite literally – isn't always worth the squeeze. But they press on. Out of a love for it, out of conviction that it's the right thing to do, and out of those moments of hope when it's enjoyed and appreciated by you.

Thank you to the producers I'm so very proud to go through this journey with, who also helped contribute to this book:

- Maria Amargiotaki and Dimitris Fragkiadoulakis, Crete, Greece
- Ana Cardoso and Paolo Morosi of Tratturo de Fronteira, Alentejo, Portugal
- Lena Puhar O'Grady of Brist, Istria, Croatia
- Christina Chrisoula of Taxidi, Crete, Greece
- Marina Segura Gómez of Peña Luna, Málaga, Spain
- Marianna Devetzoglou of Oleosophia, Corinthia, Greece
- Marije and Gui Passos of Passeite, Coimbra, Portugal
- Francesca Oliva of Agricola Oliva, Sicily, Italy
- Juan Olivares Fernández and Carolina Domínguez of Pago de Peñarrubia, Albacete, Spain
- Candice Wood and Fabrizio Ladi of Olea Prilis, Tuscany, Italy
- Brenda and Nick Wilkinson of Rio Largo Olive Estate, Breede River Valley, South Africa
- Vania Sarullo of Olio Sarullo, Sicily, Italy
- Andrea López Vericat of Sucesores de Hermanos López, Cordoba, Spain
- Edgar Morais and André Cardoso Teixeira of Soresa, Trás-os-Montes, Portugal
- Daniele and Gabriele Sapora of Olio Sapora, Riete, Italy

To the many other talented, tireless, thoughtful and dedicated producers of extra virgin olive oil who not only make an outstanding product, but also work as stewards of their land and their local community: you are so very appreciated.